OUT OF THE RUT, INTO REVIVAL

Out of the Rut, Into Revival

Dealing with Spiritual Stagnation

A. W. Tozer

Compiled by James L. Snyder

Hodder & Stoughton
LONDON SYDNEY AUCKLAND

Copyright © 1992 Christian Publications

First published in Great Britain 1993

The right of A. W. Tozer to be identified as the Author of
the Work has been asserted by the publisher in accordance with
the Copyright, Designs and Patents Act 1988.

10 9 8 7 6 5 4 3 2 1

British Library Cataloguing in Publication Data
A record for this book is available from the British Library

ISBN 0 340 72235 5

Printed and bound in Great Britain by
Clays Ltd, St Ives plc

Hodder and Stoughton Ltd
A Division of Hodder Headline PLC
338 Euston Road
London NW1 3BH

Statement from Christian Publications, USA, who commissioned this title.

This book marks the emergence of a new genre of Tozer material. Compiler James Snyder, following our mandate, has prepared a text that is as close as is reasonably possible to A.W. Tozer's spoken ministry. This is "platform Tozer." This is "Toronto Tozer." Tozer himself was a careful wordsmith who would not allow himself the liberties in print that he took as a matter of course in public speech. For Tozer purists, this text will be painful at times.

The decision for us has been this: Do we lock some of Tozer into the ongoing circulation of his taped messages alone? Or do we allow the vast treasure of the spoken Tozer to be widely circulated? Our decision has been to let Tozer speak again—in print—much as he always spoke, with good humor, with sanctified good sense, and with those bursts of prophetic insight we have come to value so highly.

CONTENTS

OUT OF THE RUT,
INTO REVIVAL

FOREWORD

I met A.W. Tozer only once, when I was serving with Youth for Christ International back in the late 50s. At my suggestion, Ted Engstrom had invited him to address our YFC Mid-Winter Convention in Chicago, knowing full well that Dr. Tozer did not totally approve of what we were doing. But we knew he was a man of God with something vitally important to say to all of God's people, and we wanted to hear him.

Well, he came (sweater and all), "nailed his 95 theses to the door" and declared to us the Word of the Lord. Some of us felt like we'd been put through an X-ray. (We didn't have laser beams and CAT scanners in those ancient days.) But God did something new and exciting in our hearts; and we look back now and realize that his ministry was a turning point in our lives.

Dr. Tozer's ministry needs neither endorsement nor promotion from me, but I am glad to recommend him to God's people. His ministry was anointed of God and his light will go on shining as long as there are believers who are weary of "rote and rut and rot," which is the theme of this collection of messages.

If the messages in this book were read and acted upon by every pastor and church member, we would have the revival for which Dr. Tozer fervently prayed and for which many of us are praying today. I confess that some of the things in this book wounded me, but it was the kind of wounding that brings healing; and I thank God for it.

Warren W. Wiersbe

CHAPTER
1

The Christian's Greatest Enemy

East of the Jordan in the territory of Moab, Moses began to expound this law, saying:

The LORD our God said to us at Horeb, "You have stayed long enough at this mountain. Break camp and advance into the hill country of the Amorites; go to all the neighboring peoples in the Arabah, in the mountains, in the western foothills, in the Negev and along the coast, to the land of the Canaanites and to Lebanon, as far as the great river, the Euphrates. See, I have given you this land. Go in and take possession of the land that the LORD swore he would give to your fathers—to Abraham, Isaac and Jacob—and to their descendants after them." (Deuteronomy 1:5–8)

In the Old Testament, the enemy that threatened Israel the most was the dictatorship of the customary. Israel became accustomed to walking around in circles and was blissfully content to stay by the safety of the mountain for a while. To put it another way, it was the psychology of the usual. God finally broke into the rut they were in and said, "You have been here long enough. It is time for you to move on."

To put Israel's experience into perspective for our benefit today, we must see that the mountain represents a spiritual experience or a spiritual state of affairs. Israel's problem was that they had given up hope of ever getting the land God had promised them. They had become satisfied with going in circles and camping in nice, comfortable places. They had come under the spell of the psychology of the routine. It kept them where they were and prevented them from getting the riches God had promised them.

If their enemy, the Edomites, would have come after them, the Israelites would have fought down to the last man and probably would have beaten the Edomites—Israel would have made progress. Instead they were twiddling their thumbs, waiting for the customary to keep on being customary.

What is the worst enemy the church faces today? This is where a lot of unreality and unconscious hypocrisy enters. Many are ready to say, "The liberals are our worst enemy." But the simple fact is that the average evangelical church does not have too much trouble with liberalism. Nobody gets up in our churches and claims that the first five books of Moses are just myths. Nobody says that the story of creation is simply religious mythology. Nobody denies that Christ walked on the water or that

He rose from the grave. Nobody gets up in our churches and claims that Jesus Christ is not the Son of God or that He isn't coming back again. Nobody denies the validity of the Scriptures. We just cannot hide behind liberalism and say that it is our worst enemy. We believe that evangelical Christians are trying to hold on to the truth given to us, the faith of our fathers, so the liberals are not our worst enemy.

Neither do we have a problem with the government. People in our country can do just about whatever they please and the government pays no attention. We can hold prayer meetings all night if we want, and the government would never bother us or question us. There is no secret police breathing down our backs watching our every move. We live in a free land, and we ought to thank God every day for that privilege.

Dictatorship of the routine

The treacherous enemy facing the church of Jesus Christ today is the dictatorship of the routine, when the routine becomes "lord" in the life of the church. Programs are organized and the prevailing conditions are accepted as normal. Anyone can predict next Sunday's service and what will happen. This seems to be the most deadly threat in the church today. When we come to the place where everything can be predicted and nobody expects anything unusual from God, we are in a rut. The routine dictates, and we can tell not only what will happen next Sunday, but what will occur next month and, if things do not improve, what will take place next year. Then we have reached the place where what has been determines what is, and what is determines what will be.

That would be perfectly all right and proper for a cemetery. Nobody expects a cemetery to do anything but conform. The greatest conformists in the world today are those who sleep out in the community cemetery. They do not bother anyone. They just lie there, and it is perfectly all right for them to do so. You can predict what everyone will do in a cemetery from the deceased right down to the people who attend a funeral there. Everyone and everything in a cemetery has accepted the routine. Nobody expects anything out of those buried in the cemetery. But the church is not a cemetery and we should expect much from it, because what has been should not be lord to tell us what is, and what is should not be ruler to tell us what will be. God's people are supposed to grow.

As long as there is growth, there is an air of unpredictability. Certainly we cannot predict exactly, but in many churches you just about can. Everybody knows just what will happen, and this has become our deadliest enemy. We blame the devil, the "last days" and anything else we can think of, but the greatest enemy is not outside of us. It is within—it is an attitude of accepting things as they are. We believe that what was must always determine what will be, and as a result we are not growing in expectation.

The progressive stages

As soon as someone begins talking like this, the Lord's people respond by getting busy. What I am talking about, however, is internal. It is a matter of the soul and mind that ultimately determines our conduct. Let me show you the progressive stages.

I begin with what I will call the *rote*. This is repetition without feeling. If someday someone would read the Scripture and believe it and would believe what is sung in the great Christian hymns, there would be a blessed spiritual revolution underway in a short time. But too many are caught up in the rote, repeating without feeling, without meaning, without wonder and without any happy surprises or expectations. In our services God cannot get in because we have it all fixed up for Him. We say, "Lord, we are going to have it this way. Now kindly bless our plans." We repeat without feeling, we repeat without meaning, we sing without wonder, and we listen without surprise. That is my description of the rote.

We go one step further and come to what I will call the *rut*, which is bondage to the rote. When we are unable to see and sense bondage to the rote, we are in a rut. For example, a man may be sick and not even know it. The doctors may have confided in the man's wife and said, "We don't want to frighten your husband, but he could drop any minute. He is critically ill, so just expect it at any moment." But the man himself does not know he is seriously ill. He goes about his business as though nothing is wrong. He may play golf or tennis, maybe even go on a hunting trip. He is sick, and yet he does not know how sick he really is. This may in fact hasten his end. Not knowing is risky business and full of danger. Spiritually speaking, the rut is bondage to the rote, and the greatest danger lies in our inability to sense or feel this bondage.

There is a third word, and I do not particularly like to use it, but the history of the church is filled with it. The word is *rot*. The church is afflicted by dry rot. This is best explained when the psychology of nonexpectation takes over and spiritual rigidity sets in, which is an inability to visualize anything better, a lack of desire for improvement.

There are many who respond by arguing, "I know lots of evangelical churches that would like to grow, and they do their best to get the crowds in. They want to grow and have contests to make their Sunday school larger." That is true, but they are trying to get people to come and share their rut. They want people to help them celebrate the rote and finally join in the rot. Because the Holy Spirit is not given a chance to work in our services, nobody is repenting, nobody is seeking God, nobody is spending a day in quiet waiting on God with open Bible seeking to mend his or her ways. Nobody is doing it—we just want more people. But more people for what? More people to come and repeat our dead services without feeling, without meaning, without wonder, without surprise? More people to join us in the bondage to the rote? For the most part, spiritual rigidity that cannot bend is too weak to know just how weak it is.

What is the church?

For clarification, what is the church? When I say that a church gets into the rote and then onto the rut and finally to the rot, what am I talking about?

For one thing, the church is not the building. A church is an assembly of individuals. There is a lot of meaningless dialogue these days about the church. It is meaningless because those engaged in the dialogue forget that a church has no separate existence. A church is not an entity in itself, but rather is composed of individual persons. It is the same error made about the state. Politicians sometimes talk about the state as though it were an entity in itself. Social workers talk about society, but society is people. So is the church. The church is made up of real people, and when they come together we have the church. Whatever the people are who make up the church, that is the kind of church it is—no worse and no better, no wiser, no holier, no more ardent and no more worshipful. To improve or change the church you must begin with individuals.

When people in the church only point to others for improvement and not to themselves, it is sure evidence that the church has come to dry rot. It is proof of three sins: the sin of self-righteousness, the sin of judgment and the sin of complacency.

When our Lord said, "One of you will betray me," thank God those disciples had enough spirituality that nobody said, "Lord, is it he?" Every one of those disciples said, "Lord, is it I?" If they would not have so responded there could not have been a Pentecost. But because they were humble enough to point the finger in their own direction the Holy Spirit fell upon them.

Self-righteousness is terrible among God's people. If we feel that we are what we ought to be, then we will remain what we are. We will not look for any change or improvement in our lives. This will quite naturally lead us to judge everyone by what we are. This is the judgment of which we must be careful. To judge others by ourselves is to create havoc in the local assembly.

Self-righteousness also leads to complacency. Complacency is a great sin and covers just about everything I have said about the rote and the rut. Some have the attitude, "Lord, I'm satisfied with my spiritual condition. I hope one of these days You will come, I will be taken up to meet You in the air and I will rule over five cities." These people cannot rule over their own houses and families, but they expect to rule over five cities. They pray spottily and sparsely, rarely attending prayer meeting, but they read their Bibles and expect to go zooming off into the blue yonder and join the Lord in the triumph of the victorious saints.

It is simply self-deception

I wonder if we are not fooling ourselves. I wonder if a lot of it is simply self-deception. I hear the voice of Jesus saying to us, "You have stayed long enough where you are. Break camp and advance into the hill country." This would be a new spiritual experience that God has for us. Everything Jesus Christ did for us we can have in this age. Victorious living, joyous living, holy living, fruitful living, wondrous, ravishing knowledge of the Triune God—all of this is ours. Power we never knew before, undreamed-of answers to prayer—this is ours. "See, I have given you this land. Go in and take possession of [it]." The Lord gave it to you in a covenant. Go take it—it's yours. It was given to Abraham, Isaac, Jacob and all their seed after. Jesus prayed, "My prayer is not for them alone. I pray also for those who will believe in me through their message" (John 17:20). That embraces all those who belong to the church of Jesus Christ.

If we call Him Lord, how dare we sit any longer in the rut! The Lord has called us to move on. But when people are in a rut, not even the angel Gabriel can help them if they will not come out of it. This is not an accusation but a suggestion. If you are not in a rut, don't get mad—somebody else is. But if you *are* in a rut you ought to get out of it.

The difference between a wooden leg and a good leg is that if you prick a wooden leg the person would never notice. The difference between a church that has dry rot and a church that is alive is that if you prick the live church it will respond. If you prick the other kind, it is already dead. The tree that stands alive has lush, green leaves. Take a knife, scar the bark deeply and the tree will bleed. It is alive. The old dead tree just stands there, a watchtower for old sentinel crows. Take your knife and dig in as far as you want to, and nothing will happen because the tree is dead.

So it is with my message. If you will get neither mad nor glad nor sad under my preaching, I know nothing can be done. But there are some who are alive, and I believe it is the majority.

CHAPTER
2

Errors in Thinking

God in His condescending love and kindness often sends a Moses, or maybe a Joshua or an Isaiah, or in latter times a Luther or Wesley to show us that the work of the Lord is not progressing. Times are bad in the kingdom and getting worse. The tendency is to settle into a rut, and we must get out of it. The time has come to arise and go on from here because God's will is as broad as the land He gave to the Israelites—"in the mountains, in the western foothills, in the Negev and along the coast, to the land of the Canaanites and to Lebanon, as far as the great river, the Euphrates" (Deuteronomy 1:7).

When God sends some preacher to say this to a congregation and the congregation is even half ready to listen to him, they say to themselves, "I think the pastor is right about this. We are in a rut, aren't we? No use fighting it. I think we ought to do something about this." Then 99.99 percent of the time the remedy prescribed will be, "Let's come together and eat

something. I know we are in a rut. We don't
see each other often enough. We ought to get to
know each other better, so let's come together
and eat something." I have no objection to fellowship, but it is not the answer to what is
wrong with us.

Instead of eating, someone may suggest,
"Let's make plans to go somewhere." This is
another way we Protestants have of curing all
the sores of Job, all the leprosy and everything
that is wrong with us. We either get together to
eat our way out or else we travel and get out of
it.

Another person might say, "Let's come
together and do something religious. The
church is in pretty bad shape. Morale is low,
and things are not the way they should be. We
are running pretty much in a circle. Let's get
together and do something." This is activism.

Someone else says, "Let's form a committee
to consider it." The Baptist preacher Dr. Vance
Havner says, "A committee is a company of the
incompetent chosen by the unwilling to do the
unnecessary." Perhaps he stated that a little too
radically. There are some things committees
can do, and then there are some things committees cannot do.

I am quite sure that when the man of God
thundered, "You have stayed long enough in
this place. You are going around in circles. Get
you out and take what is given to you by the
hand of your God," nobody got up and said,

"Mr. Chairman, let's eat something." Eating probably would not have helped. I am quite certain that they did not get up and say, "Let's take a trip," or "Let's start another club." Starting a club is another reaction we have when we find ourselves in a rut and realize we are no taller than we were five years ago; we are no farther along than we were five years ago; we don't know any more than we did five years ago; we are no holier than we were five years ago. We simply met ourselves coming around.

If a song could be worn out, we have worn out the same old song: "Revive us again, fill each heart with Thy love." We have sung that one and nobody means it—nobody will pay the price. But we go around and around, and all we see is the other fellow's heels just ahead of us. All the fellow behind us sees is our heels. We go around and around the circle, and somebody says, "Let's start a club now."

Misunderstood the problem

Fellowship, committees and clubs are all right under the right circumstances, but this kind of an answer to that kind of a problem presupposes that those who give the answer have misunderstood the problem. There are three things they misunderstand.

First, they misunderstand the nature of Christian faith. Christian faith is inward, not outward. It is of the spirit and not of the flesh. The kingdom of God is within you, Christ dwells in your heart, and "Christ in you, the hope of glory" (Colossians 1:27) is the burning core of the Christian faith. So Christianity, the true Christian faith, is inward in nature—we are to be inwardly Christians. It is inside, somewhere in the spirit, soul and heart—the inner person—that we get into the rut. Because the problem is inward, it is ridiculous to say, "All right. The inner person, the spirit of me, the inner shrine of me, is in a rut. It isn't where it ought to be, so let's eat something."

The nature of the church

Second, they misunderstand the nature of the church. You see, the church is a body of individuals united in Christ but having separate individual responsibilities. Thus the body is improved only as we improve the individuals that compose the body. The Holy Spirit fell at Pentecost on approximately 120 people. But it fell on them individually, and if any had hardened themselves they would have been passed over.

Each person is born individually even if he or she is one of a set of triplets. We are born one at a time, and we die one at a time; we face judgment one at a time and, if we as Christians are sick, we will be cured one at a time. The body is composed of individuals, and to say, "All right, let's form committees to look into it," is trying to do by a dozen people what God cannot do for one person—fix the problem by external means. It does not work, and it will never work. Because we misunderstand the nature of the church, we misunderstand how to solve the problem.

What is wrong with them

Third, they misunderstand what is wrong with them. You cannot cure a weak member by prescribing a certain diet. You can eat caviar and hummingbird tongue until the sun goes down, but it will not help you, because that is not what is wrong with you. Somebody else says, "Let's take a trip." Take your trip—it is all right. Try not to get killed on the way. But remember, that is not what is wrong with you. Somebody else says, "Let's start a committee to handle it." The lack of a committee is not what is wrong with you, either. You are missing the nature of true Christian faith, for true Christianity is inward, and what is wrong cannot be reached by these external means.

Now suppose we are ready to admit that we are in a rut. You say, "Well, what is the church doing?" I don't know, because it is the individual that matters. You see, the church is composed of this fellow that lives out here a little way and those two people who live out there in Scarboro and the five who live in Rexdale and the seven who live up in Willowdale and the 14 who live out east. That is the church. What the church does is what the individuals do. How well or how sick the church is depends on how well or how sick the individuals are. In other words, it depends upon how you are.

We must come to the Lord and say, "Oh Lord, what do I still lack? I have some things, Lord, but what do I lack? Or what is it that I ought to get rid of? How do I compare with what I should be? How do I know what I should be?"

In Matthew 5:3–10 we read:

> Blessed are the poor in spirit,
>   for theirs is the kingdom of heaven.
> Blessed are those who mourn,
>   for they will be comforted.
> Blessed are the meek,
>   for they will inherit the earth.
> Blessed are those who hunger and thirst
>   for righteousness,
>   for they will be filled.
> Blessed are the merciful,
>   for they will be shown mercy.
> Blessed are the pure in heart,
>   for they will see God.
> Blessed are the peacemakers,
>   for they will be called sons of God.
> Blessed are those who are persecuted
>   because of righteousness,
>   for theirs is the kingdom of heaven.

That is what we ought to be. This passage tells us what a true Christian should be like. Go on to the epistles and see what the man of God has to say there. In Ephesians 4:26–5:2 he says,

> "In your anger do not sin": Do not let the sun go down while you are still angry, and do not give the devil a foothold. He who has been stealing must steal no longer, but must work, doing something useful with his own hands, that he may have something to share with those in need.
>
> Do not let any unwholesome talk come out of your mouths, but only what is helpful for building others up according to their needs, that it may benefit those who listen. And do not grieve the Holy Spirit of God, with whom you were sealed for the day of redemption. Get rid of all bitterness, rage and anger, brawling and slander, along with every form of malice. Be kind and compassionate to one another, forgiving each other, just as in Christ God forgave you. Be imitators of God, therefore, as dearly loved children and live a life of love, just as Christ loved us and gave himself up for us as a fragrant offering and sacrifice to God.

This is what we ought to be. This is the way we ought to be living. When we say, "Lord, what do I still lack?" the Holy Spirit answers, "This is what you lack."

Remember, we are compared with what we

could be, not just what we *should* be. God being who He is, and Jesus Christ being His risen and all-powerful Son, anything we ought to be we can be. Anything that God has declared that we should be we can be.

In the wonderful book of Romans, perhaps the greatest and most profound book in the Bible, chapter 7 tells us of a man who is struggling and wanting to be something that he feels he cannot be. Finally he gives up and says, "What a wretched man I am! Who will rescue me from this body of death?" (verse 24). Immediately, Paul says, "Thanks be to God! . . . because through Christ Jesus the law of the Spirit of life set me free from the law of sin and death" (25; 8:2).

In Galatians 5:22–23 we read, "But the fruit of the Spirit is love, joy, peace, patience, kindness, goodness, faithfulness, gentleness and self-control. Against such things there is no law." That is what we ought to be and what we can be. Now compare that with what we are. If we compare what we ought to be and could be with what we are, and we don't see that we are in a rut and we are not concerned, then one of three things may be wrong.

We may not be converted

First, we may not be converted at all. I am convinced that many evangelicals are not truly and soundly converted. Among the evangelicals it is entirely possible to come into membership, to ooze in by osmosis, to leak through the cells of the church and never know what it means to be born of the Spirit and washed in the blood. A great deal that passes for the deeper life is nothing more or less than basic Christianity. There is nothing deeper about it, and it is where we should have been from the start. We should have been happy, joyous, victorious Christians walking in the Holy Spirit and not fulfilling the lusts of the flesh. Instead we have been chasing each other around the perpetual mountain.

What we need is what the old Methodists called a sound conversion. There is a difference between conversion and a sound conversion. People who have never been soundly converted do not have the Spirit to enlighten them. When they read the Sermon on the Mount or the teaching passages of the epistles that tell them how to live or the doctrinal passages that tell how they can live, they are unaffected. The Spirit who wrote them is not witnessing in their hearts because they have not been born of the Spirit. That often happens.

People clean up, throw away their pipes, start to pay their bills and live right and then say, "I want to join the church." So we question them, "Do you believe that Christ is the Son of God?"

"Yes," they reply.

"Do you believe He rose from the dead?"

"Yes."

"Do you believe He is coming again?"

"Yes, I do."

Well, so does the devil and he trembles.

People get into the church who are not converted at all. We are so tenderhearted, sentimental and eager that we get them on any grounds at all, if they just say the right words for us. But maybe some of these people have never been converted in the first place.

Second, people may not be concerned about the rut because of sin they have committed. Perhaps they have been regenerated but have sinned against light too often, so the light has become darkness. That often happens.

I don't say these people are lost, but I do say that they are in a terrible state. Only the power and grace of God working within them can help. I think there are lots of people like that. They have been regenerated, but they have become busy with their real estate office or their store. Many have said, "Well, I'd like to come to your church, Reverend, but I have to keep my store open seven days a week." They cannot serve God because they do not have time to serve Him. They will have time to die, but they do not have time to serve God.

Third, some people are so self-righteous that they are impervious to any work of the Holy Spirit. They cannot be cured of their blindness because they think they see. The Pharisees never got under conviction. They crucified Christ, they hated the Son of God, but they never got under conviction. They had ordered their religious life so as to be impervious to the arrows of the Holy Spirit. The adulterous woman could fall at the feet of Jesus, the tax collector who knew he had been crooked could run to the feet of Jesus to ask for help, and the poor came from everywhere to say, "What must I do?" They could come, but the Pharisees never did. They never got under conviction, and in hell I suppose they are still fighting and saying they are right.

If people judge what they could be and ought to be with what they are and can still go home and have a good night's rest, shrugging it off, perhaps they have never been converted. Maybe they have sinned against light until they are temporarily under a terrible cloud of God's judgment. Or maybe they are so self-righteous that they cannot get under conviction.

There is hope

But if they are concerned, wounded by the Spirit's sword and are deeply dissatisfied with the religious rut, there is hope. Remember, complacency is a deadly foe. Complacency is as great a foe as any other carnal malady, any other fleshly manifestation. To be complacent is to have no desire to get anywhere.

There was a celebrated Englishman who sat with a friend once, watching and listening to a philharmonic orchestra. As they listened, the Englishman watched a man playing second violin. He was playing it well, but he was second violin. The Englishman said to his friend, "See that man there playing second violin? If I were playing second violin in that orchestra, do you know what I would do? I would never rest day or night until I was playing first violin. And then I would never give myself rest day or night until I was directing that orchestra. When I got to be director I would never rest until I had become a composer. And when I got to composing music for the orchestra I would never give myself rest until I was the best composer in England."

Children of the world are wiser

The children of the world are sometimes wiser than the children of light. We have been offered not the directorship of a great orchestra, but glory and truth unsearchable. We have been offered the face of God and the glory of Christ. We have been offered holiness and righteousness and indwelling by the Spirit. We can have our prayers answered and have hell fear us because we have a hold on God who invites us to draw on His omnipotence. We are offered all this, and yet we sit and play second violin without ambition.

Israel was once in that condition, and an old prophet with shining eyes came to them and said,

Woe to you who are complacent in Zion,

and to you who feel secure on Mount
    Samaria, . . .
You put off the evil day
    and bring near a reign of terror.
You lie on beds inlaid with ivory
    and lounge on your couches.
You dine on choice lambs
    and fattened calves.
You strum away on your harps like David
    and improvise on musical instruments.
You drink wine by the bowlful
    and use the finest lotions,
    but you do not grieve over the ruin
        of Joseph.
Therefore you will be among the first
    to go into exile. (Amos 6:1–7)

Israel was in a rut, and they did not want anybody disturbing their calm. They liked music and food and beds of ivory, and they anointed themselves with ointment. They had everything that we call sumptuous living. But they were not grieved at the affliction of Israel. They didn't care.

Let us not rest upon beds of ivory. By the grace of God let us begin to grieve a bit for the affliction of Joseph and be anxious and bothered in the Holy Spirit for the state the church is in.

Awakened Out
of Sleep

My aim is to awaken some from the rut. I know it is impossible to awaken everybody, but I hope to awaken some. I use the word *awaken* here advisedly and carefully because the Bible contains significant teaching gathered around the word *sleep*.

There is first of all *natural sleep*. "He grants sleep to those he loves" (Psalm 127:2). "I will lie down and sleep in peace, for you alone, O LORD, make me dwell in safety" (Psalm 4:8).

Our Lord Himself slept in the boat. Natural sleep is scarcely worth mentioning because it is the gift of God to us. We sleep when we can, and when we cannot something is wrong. Natural sleep is innocent, provided we are not sleeping when we should be doing something else. If we sleep when we should be praying, then it is not innocent, though it is natural. Natural sleep is innocent when "He grants sleep to those he loves." But, for instance, those disciples who slept when they should have been awake praying with Jesus, had natural, but not innocent, sleep. However, we will waive aside natural sleep because that is not what we are going to study now.

I am thinking of *moral sleep* and *spiritual sleep*. Moral sleep is suggested in First Corinthians 15:34, "Awake to righteousness and sin not" (KJV). There is such a thing as moral sleep. It is entirely possible to be displeasing God and grieving the Holy Spirit by being asleep morally; that is, by permitting what should not be allowed. Most people do not want to hear this. They want something added to what they have. They do not want to be told that they are permitting something that should not be allowed. In other words, they are doing what they should not be doing.

But you ask, "Is that true of Christians? Do you believe that many Christians are doing this?" I have no hesitation in saying that all the symptoms in the church today point to Christians doing things they should not be doing and failing to do what they should be doing. That is the positive and the negative—sins of commission, sins of omission. To be unaware of these sins is to be morally asleep.

Sudden awakening

When the Bible says "Awake to righteousness and sin not," it indicates the possibility of a sudden awakening, like when an alarm clock going off rouses you out of sleep. There is such a thing as being asleep and suddenly being wakened, and this is surprising to people. People often say, "You know, I was living a life displeasing to God. I was a church member, but though I didn't know it, I was displeasing to God. My life wasn't right. Then suddenly I was wakened by God. It was a surprise."

Not only is awakening a surprise, but it can be disconcerting, as when you are driving to some particular destination. You have decided which way you are going and where you are on the map. Then you find landmarks that indicate you are just plain wrong. You have been going the wrong way. It is not only a surprise to you, but it is disconcerting because you lose self-confidence.

People who are awakened from moral sleep say, "Well, what's the matter with me? I've been living a life that's been displeasing to God, and I simply did not know it. 'Surely the LORD is in this place, and I was not aware of it. . . . This is none other than the house of God; this is the gate of heaven' " (Genesis 28:16–17). Jacob must have been rather disconcerted when he awoke and found that he had been in the presence of God all the time, but he had been asleep. He was not morally dead; he was not cut off from the covenant—he was merely asleep.

There is also *spiritual sleep*. Notice Ephesians 5:14: "Wake up, O sleeper, rise from the dead." This verse is often spoken to sinners, but it was not written to sinners. Ephesians was never written to sinners. It is not a message to sinners at all, but a message to one of the best churches in the New Testament. Yet the writer says, "Wake up, O sleeper, rise from the dead, and Christ will shine on you." Some of the Ephesians were in a somnolent condition; that is, they were morally good but unenlightened. They were religious but unanointed. It is perfectly possible for a good, faithful, loyal church member to be spiritually asleep—being in a spiritual state that parallels natural sleep.

When your husband, your wife, your child, your relative, your friend or you go to sleep tonight, the fact that you are unconscious and out of the running for a while is not bothering you. You know that normally you will wake up again. You are not dead, but you are cut off from your environment, all but that which is reflex—breathing and a few other things. Likewise it is possible to be a Christian, to be in the church and yet be asleep spiritually. Then you have to be wakened suddenly. You will probably be ashamed of yourself, angry with yourself, frustrated and disconcerted and say, "What's the matter with me? All this time I was almost awake, but not quite."

Bulk of Christians asleep

What is the present condition of the evangelical church? The bulk of Christians are asleep. I do not mean that the bulk of Christians who come to evangelical churches are not converted, because if I meant that I would say they were dead and never had been born again. But I say they are asleep. It is possible to be morally asleep and yet intellectually, mentally and physically alert. It is possible to be spiritually asleep yet mentally, intellectually, physically and theologically alert.

The present condition is that we are asleep. These sleeping Christians do two things that God must grieve over. One is that they control church affairs. We are democratic, and if we do not like a pastor we give him the bounce or pray that he will get another call. Then when the time comes we vote in whom we want and vote out whom we do not want. Church people control church affairs because they are intellectually, mentally and physically awake, but they may be morally and spiritually asleep. That is, they are so far down in the rut that they do not see up.

Many people who are asleep control church affairs. It gets into whole conferences. Representatives will meet at the expense of the local church people. They will read minutes and pass resolutions, but they are asleep. You know they are asleep by the way they talk as soon as the benediction is pronounced and they have adjourned. You know they are asleep by their conduct, the things they are interested in or lack interest in, yet they control church affairs.

The second thing sleeping Christians do is set

the standards for new Christians. When you bring in a newly converted Christian, he or she automatically takes on the coloration, general mood and temperature of the solemn seats around him or her. Pretty soon he or she is where they are, and once again there are no good examples of the Christian life.

Of course, people resent any word reflecting on them, but every once in a while there appears an awakened soul. Some way or another this person got awake. Somehow God Almighty wakened him or her, whether by the crowing of the rooster or by the braying of Balaam's donkey. This person ceases to be mediocre and somnolent and becomes a blazing, shining light. And then the sleeping saints pay to have him or her come and do their work for them. They send people like this out to South Africa or the Far East to do their work for them. Meanwhile they stay home and sleep spiritually, and earn the money, because they are intellectually and physically awake to send them.

When one of these people dies, they write the story of his or her life and may even go so far as to take up a collection to put up a little library in the person's memory. They could call it the "Awakened Saint Memorial." But they are very careful not to be awakened themselves. They are careful and perfectly happy to talk about how wonderful Robert Jaffray was, but they will not pay Jaffray's price. They can talk endlessly about wonderful Dr. A.B. Simpson, but they will not go Simpson's way. They are careful not to follow the person whose life they write about and whose memorial they erect.

But this is what Christianity is all about: the wakened soul, the morally and spiritually wakened. God, who seems so far away, suddenly becomes close. God who had been all out of focus, a blur, now is seen to be the Son of Righteousness in clear sight, with healing in His wings.

CHAPTER
4

The Church
in the Rut

*For I do not want you to be ignorant of the fact,
brothers, that our forefathers were all under the
cloud and that they all passed through the sea.
They were all baptized into Moses in the cloud and
in the sea. They all ate the same spiritual food and
drank the same spiritual drink; for they drank from
the spiritual rock that accompanied them, and that
rock was Christ. Nevertheless, God was not
pleased with most of them; their bodies were scat-
tered over the desert.*

*Now these things occurred as examples to keep
us from setting our hearts on evil things as they
did. Do not be idolaters, as some of them were; as it
is written: "The people sat down to eat and drink
and got up to indulge in pagan revelry." We
should not commit sexual immorality, as some of
them did—and in one day twenty-three thousand
of them died. We should not test the Lord, as some
of them did—and were killed by snakes. And do
not grumble, as some of them did—and were killed
by the destroying angel.*

*These things happened to them as examples and
were written down as warnings for us, on whom
the fulfillment of the ages has come. So, if you*

think you are standing firm, be careful that you don't fall! (1 Corinthians 10:1–12)

The LORD our God said to us at Horeb, "You have stayed long enough at this mountain. Break camp and advance into the hill country of the Amorites; go to all the neighboring peoples in the Arabah, in the mountains, in the western foothills, in the Negev and along the coast, to the land of the Canaanites and to Lebanon, as far as the great river, the Euphrates. See, I have given you this land. Go in and take possession of the land that the LORD swore he would give to your fathers—to Abraham, Isaac and Jacob—and to their descendants after them." (Deuteronomy 1:6–8)

Churches get in ruts only because individuals get in ruts. It is impossible that the church should do anything that individuals do not do. It is impossible that we should make any progress except as made by individuals. It is impossible there should be any regress unless individual Christians go backward.

Think about people who find themselves in religious ruts. They discover a number of things about themselves. They will find that they are getting older but not getting any holier. Time is their enemy, not their friend. The time they trusted and looked to is betraying them, for they often said to themselves, "The passing of time will help me. I know some good old saints, so as I get older I'll get holier and better. Time will help me, purify me and revive me." They said that the year before last, but they were not helped any last year. Time betrayed them. They were not any better last year than they had been the year before.

Nevertheless, last year they said, "Next year surely I'll make some progress. I'll get out of this rut. I'll go forward with God." That would have been this year, but this year they are not any further along than they were last year or the year before. This year they might be saying, "Well, time is my friend. Time will help me. I'm getting older, and next year I will make progress." I say to you that the people in the religious rut are getting older, but they are not getting any holier. Time, which they have trusted to be their friend, is betraying them and proving to be their enemy.

Time is doing something else to them: it is increasing their indifference to spiritual things. The signal that God used to be able to get through to them easily is now getting fainter and fading away. Once in a while on good days they can still hear it.

You know how it is when you travel away from a city like Toronto. You have your radio on to get the news or just to listen to music. You want to listen to it, but as you move away the station gets fainter. The signal is still reasonably clear, but it is fainter. And then you get into a pocket where you do not hear it at all. You say to yourself, "Well, that station is fading out." Then suddenly it comes on again. "Well," you might say, "we're hearing it again." But it is still very faint. When you get far enough away from the city you do not hear it at all.

Dull religious feelings

That is exactly what people in ruts find out about themselves. They discover that the passing of time tends to dull their religious feelings, and the signal that used to be quite clear is fading out. Then they worry a little and say, "The signal is gone. I'll have to do something." Suddenly it comes on again and they hear it a little and say, "Oh, it's not so bad after all." They are just in a favorable pocket—perhaps some new preacher has come to town. They think they are hearing the voice again, and they are, a little bit. But it is not long until they are out of range and cannot hear it anymore. Time has increased their indifference to spiritual things and dulled their religious feelings, continually making them harder to change.

Change is one of the ingredients of Christianity. If people could not change, the gospel would be absolutely meaningless. If the Lord would say, "Believe on the Lord Jesus Christ; repent and believe," and a person could not repent or believe, the gospel would be meaningless. The fact that people can change is the only hope they have. If they could not change, there would be no reason to preach to them that they must change. And yet we are sent to preach that people should change, meaning they should repent. They should turn from darkness to light. They should turn from idols to God. They should change. This is absolutely necessary, a vital ingredient in the spiritual life.

People who are in the rut, the circular grave, find that it is getting harder for them to change. They used to have spells when they were emotionally moved. Their wills got over on the side of God, and they really meant to make themselves into good Christians by the grace of God. But those times are getting fewer. They cannot afford to wait and say, "Oh, well, I will do it next Thanksgiving. I'll do it when I come home from vacation." No, they will either do it now or they will not do it at all.

There comes a time when they must make a change. If they do not make it, they never will. Time is stealing away their days of opportunity to make it. They began with a given number of days, and they have already used up so many days. But the tragedy is that they do not know how many remain. They do not know how many they have left because they do not know how many they had to start with. While they could count the number of days they have been on the earth, they do not know how that stacks up to the number accorded them, so they do not know where they are. They only know that the days are doing what the poet said about the leaves. "The leaves of life keep falling one by one."

A beautiful sugar maple stands in front of our house up on Old Orchard Grove. It is one of the greenest trees I have ever seen. It hangs on to its leaves a long time, and then sometime in October I notice some leaves are missing and say to myself, "Oh well, there is still a mass of leaves. I do not need to worry." The next day I notice there are not as many leaves, and then I begin to notice some branches beginning to show. Before the snow flies there is not a leaf left. People in the rut never know when the last leaves are falling for them.

Reasons for the rut

Why are people in the rut? There are several possibilities. They may never have been truly converted at all, and this is one of our great problems now. We have a dozen ways of getting people into the kingdom of God, when the Lord said there was only one. They leak in, ooze in, come in by osmosis and get in by marriage—just get in by any kind of way. But there is only one true way. When people find that after being in the church for years they are not making much progress, they ought to examine themselves and wonder whether they have been truly converted. True conversion means radical repentance, a changed life, conscious forgiveness of sin and a spiritual rebirth. Genuinely converted people, as the old

Methodists said, had a radical repentance, which eventuated in a changed life. Then there came a consciousness of forgiveness of sins and a spiritual rebirth. People in the rut may never have had that at all.

Maybe they have been abandoned to the devil as a severe disciplinary measure to keep them out of hell.

> When you are assembled in the name of our Lord Jesus and I am with you in spirit, and the power of our Lord Jesus is present, hand this man over to Satan, so that the sinful nature may be destroyed and his spirit saved on the day of the Lord. (1 Corinthians 5:4–5)

> A man ought to examine himself before he eats of the bread and drinks of the cup. For anyone who eats and drinks without recognizing the body of the Lord eats and drinks judgment on himself. That is why many among you are weak and sick, and a number of you have fallen asleep. But if we judged ourselves, we would not come under judgment. When we are judged by the Lord, we are being disciplined so that we will not be condemned with the world. (11:28–32)

People in the circular grave, who are getting older without getting holier, may have been abandoned to the devil because of two things—some fleshly sins (1 Corinthians 5) or grave irreverence at the communion table (1 Corinthians 11).

Protestants are altogether too much inclined to take things for granted. We laugh at those on the other side of the ecclesiastical fence because they bow and scrape and kowtow in the presence of the church. But we lack reverence—not because we are free in the gospel, but because God is absent, and we have no sense of His presence. We sometimes come to the communion table in a moral and spiritual state totally unfit for receiving communion, and yet we take it. Paul said, "We are judged by the Lord, we are being disciplined so that we will not be condemned with the world."

Sin is the cause

It is almost certain that sin is the cause of the rut, the circular grave in which so many people find themselves. Since only sin offends God, and sin is extremely deceitful, it can be present doing its deadly work while the people may not be not aware of it at all until it is called to their attention. There are several kinds of sin that cause the rut. First is the sin of omission, an act left undone that should have been done. Next is the sin of commission, which is an act displeasing to God, to the Holy Spirit. There is also sin of the flesh. The world may approve of sin of the flesh, and even churches and pastors may permit it. It is astonishing what preachers will joke about with their congregations, laugh off and put up with. Maybe pastors permit it, or laugh it off at least, and say, "Oh well, you can't be too holy, too angelic in this world." But the Holy Spirit is grieved by it.

So the people move around their circular grave not hearing the voice much any more. They used to hear it, "Get up, get up. You've been in this place long enough. Get up! Move! There's the land before you—I've given it to you. It's all in the covenant; it is all in the purchase of the blood. It is all yours. Get up and move toward me. Move toward the holy place and the holy land and your possessions. Victory and deliverance and power in prayer—it is all yours. Rise up and take it." They once heard that signal coming strongly to them, but it is not coming so strongly any more. The Holy Spirit is grieved and does not talk so much. And the people move around in their circular grave.

Perhaps they have committed sins of the mind. "Society," said Emerson, "is in conspiracy to make every man like every other man." But what he did not say was that society is in a conspiracy to make every man ungodly in his thinking. By "ungodly" I do not mean that he likes pornographic pictures or that he stands on the corner of a street on a windy day and watches the girls go by. That is only one facet of wrongdoing or sin. Wrong ambition, love of money, overappreciation of earthly things, jealousy and envy all fit in to make a web, and society is teaching us and conditioning our minds to think sinfully. This begins in the cradle.

Thoughts require much prayer

To think God's thoughts requires much prayer. If you do not pray much, you are not thinking God's thoughts. If you do not read your Bible much and often and reverently, you are not thinking God's thoughts. Those thoughts you are having—and your head buzzes with them all day long and into the night—are earthly thoughts—thoughts of a fallen race. They are the thoughts of a lost society. They should not be our thoughts. Paul said, "Let this mind be in you, which was also in Christ Jesus" (Philippians 2:5 KJV).

There also has to be a lot of meditation. We ought to learn to live in our Bibles. Get one with print big enough to read so it does not punish your eyes. Look around until you find a good one, and then learn to love it. Begin with the Gospel of John, then read the Psalms. Isaiah is another great book to help you and lift you. When you feel you want to do it, go on to Romans and Hebrews and some of the deeper theological books. But get into the Bible. Do not just read the little passages you like, but in the course of a year or two see that you read it through. Your thoughts will one day come up before God's judgment. We are responsible for our premeditative thoughts. They make our mind a temple where God can dwell with pleasure, or they make our mind a stable where Christ is angry, ties a rope and drives out the cattle. It is all up to us.

What should you then do? Examine yourself. Have you found yourself in that awful circular grave, not making any spiritual progress? Have you found that the passing of time upon which you have leaned so heavily has become a broken reed and is not helping you at all?

The philosopher Socrates said, "An unexamined life is not worth living." If a common philosopher could think that, how much more we Christians ought to listen to the Holy Spirit when He says, "Examine yourself." An unexamined Christian lies like an unattended garden. Let your garden go unattended for a few months, and you will not have roses and tomatoes but weeds. An unexamined Christian life is like an unkempt house. Lock your house up as tight as you will and leave it long enough, and when you come back you will not believe the dirt that got in from somewhere. An unexamined Christian is like an untaught child. A child that is not taught will be a little savage. It takes examination, teaching, instruction, discipline, caring, tending, weeding and cultivating to keep the life right.

I do not want to leave you on a low note. I am

trying to wake you, not discourage you. There is not a reason in the world for you to be discouraged. Suppose there were an elixir of life that could cure any disease anyone could have, and it was sold down at the corner, and you could buy it for a nickel a bottle. It was the magic elixir of life that would make anybody healthy.

Then suppose that I found an old fellow sitting on a bench and I went and sat down beside him. I noticed by looking at him that he had high blood pressure. I could tell it by the veins that stood out on his forehead. I began to try to tell him, "You have lived long enough on this bench. Get up; there's something better for you," and he began to resist me. Then I would have to preach a whole series of sermons to him to get him to know how sick he is, when just down the street a little way was the cure for what was wrong with him.

That is precisely where we are in the church. You have to work on people for weeks to get them to see that they are in a rut. It would be cruel to do if there was not a remedy. But the justice of God is on the side of the confessing sinner. "If we confess our sins, he is faithful and just and will forgive us our sins and purify us from all unrighteousness" (1 John 1:9). Because Jesus Christ died, because He was God and because He was man, His atonement was absolutely and fully efficacious. All of the attributes of God are on the side of the person who confesses his or her sin and turns and runs to the feet of Jesus.

"My dear children, I write this to you so that you will not sin. But if anybody does sin, we have one who speaks to the Father in our defense—Jesus Christ, the Righteous One. He is the atoning sacrifice for our sins, and not only for ours but also for the sins of the whole world" (2:1-2). There is the elixir. There is the cure. That is only one little passage, and of course similar ones are all over the New Testament. The blood is shed for us. God pardons and forgives for Christ's sake. The Holy Spirit is here to take the things of Christ and make them real to us. There is nothing, not even the devil himself, that can hinder the confessing sinner.

CHAPTER
5

Getting Out
of the Rut

*Therefore, my dear friends, as you have always
obeyed—not only in my presence, but now much
more in my absence—continue to work out your
salvation with fear and trembling, for it is God
who works in you to will and to act according to
his good purpose. (Philippians 2:12–13)*

The Holy Spirit in this passage is saying
two things: God works in you to will, but
you are to work with God in working it out.
God works in you—that is, God is always previous. God is the aggressor. God saw you in
the rut and wanted you to get out of it. He
thought of it first, not you. The impulse to
know God came from Him and not from you.
God works first, and because God works we
are to work with Him. We are therefore to dismiss all doubts and all morbid humility.

It is entirely possible to be so humble, in a
sick kind of way, that you paralyze yourself

46

and get nowhere. For instance, you say to yourself, "That man has been preaching about getting out of the religious rut. While I haven't agreed with everything, I have been feeling that I am in a rut and that I ought to get out. This circular grave is getting deeper every year of my life, and I can hardly see out of it. Give me four or five more years and you'll look right over me and not know I'm here. I need help. But I wonder if God will help me."

That is morbid humility. If you knew the truth, you would know that you would have gone on around in that circular grave until you had worn your way down to China and never thought of getting out of it. The very fact that you want out is proof that God has been working in you to will to get out. And if God worked in you to want to get out, then when you ask Him to get you out, do you suppose He would *not* help you out? Would God put an impulse in your heart and then refuse to accept your prayer when you came in answer to that impulse? Would a mother bring a hungry baby to the table, prepare his food and then when he let out his happy little yell and stretched out his hand, pull it away? Would she say, "You're no good. You've never done anything anyhow"?

Grant the baby your intelligence, and this is what the baby would say to himself: "I am now eight months old, and I haven't helped my mother at all. I've been bad sometimes. I've kept her up at night. I am obviously no good. I'm not making any contribution to society. Why should I think that mother is going to feed me?"

In the meantime, mother is begging the child to eat, but the baby says there is no use. Now that would be morbid humility. Of course, no baby would have that much intelligence. He would just grab for what was in front of him. That is exactly what God wants you to do. If God had not put it in your heart to want His blessing, you would not have wanted it.

Work with Him

The fact that you are ready to listen to this kind of message indicates that God has been previous in your life. Therefore, you must work with Him in harmonious cooperation so He can work in you and for you and through you.

People use the word *fanatic* whenever you get a little bit joyful about the Lord. They say you are a fanatic. Webster says that a fanatic is somebody who is too enthusiastic about religion, as if you could be too enthusiastic about religion. John Wesley said, "A fanatic is one who seeks desirable ends but ignores constituted means."

Suppose a farmer boy with his blue jeans, torn shirt and tattered straw hat wants to get a fish. His mother says, "Why don't you go down and catch a couple of trout, son." So he goes down by the creek. It is a beautiful day, the sun is shining and the cows are standing deep in the water under the shade trees. So the boy pulls off a stalk of grass and begins to nibble on it, and he starts wondering about those fish. He says to himself, "I remember the pastor said if we want anything to pray for it." In the meantime the fish are breaking the surface begging to be caught. But there he is praying, "Lord, send me some fish." He can pray until he dies and he will never have any fish. The Lord put intelligence in his head and gave him what we call constituted means. The farm boy takes a branch from a tree, ties on an ordinary piece of cord, puts a bent pin on the end and throws the hook with a worm on it into the stream. The fish will take it.

Would it be proper for the farm boy to be pious and pray for fish or to throw in his hook and pull out fish? Everybody knows that if a farm boy addresses the Almighty God in a loud voice asking for fish when the fish are breaking the surface begging to be caught, something is wrong. He is a fanatic—he is trying to get a desirable end, but he is ignoring constituted means.

Now suppose his father attends the church where they have a fine pastor who tells them that if they pray they will get what they pray for. He wants potatoes in the springtime, and he says, "I'd like to have a good field of potatoes this year. I really need them." So he gets down on his knees and every day he spends time praying for potatoes while it gets too late to plant them. There are potatoes down in the basement waiting to be cut and planted. They are already stretching out their long roots toward the sunlight. They are begging for him to use the constituted means. Plow the field. Get it in shape. Cut the potatoes and plant them. Go around and keep the weeds down, and come back and take out a great crop. These are constituted means.

Suppose the woman of the house wants some ducks. She just has a yen for a hat full of ducklings. She loves little ducklings, so she wants some. Down on her knees she prays for ducks day and night. She is not using constituted means. The way you get ducks is to find fertile duck eggs and put them under a hen. Four weeks and they are out.

Desirable ends, constituted means

A fanatic is somebody seeking desirable ends but ignoring constituted means. Seeking to get out of the religious rut is a desirable end. It is right and it is in the will of God. But trying to do it in a manner that is not according to God's constituted means is all wrong and gets us nowhere.

When they want to get blessed, some people try getting worked up psychologically. There are some who, while they have not studied psychology, are master psychologists. They know how to manipulate audiences, knowing when to lower their voices and when to raise them, when to make them sound very sad and all the rest. They know how to get people all worked up.

I sat listening to a preacher one time, and right across from me was a young woman, maybe 22 or 23 years old. The only reason I noticed her was that she had on a pair of glass shoes. The preacher went on preaching, and he never, as far as I remember, said anything about the Lord. But he did tell us all about his father and his mother and how his father left home and the whole story. I watched this woman, then I would watch the preacher and then look at her again. At first she could not have cared less, but slowly he got hold of her. When it came to the point where the evangelist said in a tremulous voice that every time he faced an audience he hoped that his old father might be there, the girl broke down and went to pieces. From that moment she was eating out of his hand. He knew how to handle her psychologically. He got her, and she would have done anything for him.

Some people try group dynamics. We all sit around together and practice togetherness, and by practicing togetherness we finally work up some spirituality.

What is needed is some old-fashioned, salty horse sense. I am sure there are 189 mules in the state of Missouri that have more sense than a lot of the preachers who are trying to teach people how to get the blessing of God in some way other than by the constituted means. When you get people all broken up, dabbing at their eyes and shaking, what is the result? It does not bring them any closer to God. It does not make them love God any better, in accordance with the first commandment. Nor does it give any greater love for neighbors, which is the second commandment. It does not prepare them to live fruitfully on earth. It does not prepare them to die victoriously, and it does not guarantee that they will be with the Lord at last.

The Lord's constituted means

The Lord has constituted means. Jesus said in the Gospel of John, "Whoever has my commands and obeys them, he is the one who loves me" (John 14:21a). Anybody can understand that, even the teacher of group dynamics.

> He who loves me will be loved by my Father, and I too will love him and show myself to him.
> If anyone loves me, he will obey my teaching. My Father will love him, and we will come to him and make our home with him. He who does not love me will not obey my teaching. These words you hear are not my own; they belong to the Father who sent me. (14:21b, 23–24)

What our Lord taught was this: when we obey the words of Jesus, in faith and in love proving that we love Him, He shows Himself to us. There are two subjects acting here—*we* and *He*. When *we* obey His Word *we* prove that *we* love Him, and *He* shows Himself to us. Who is this *He* that I am talking about? Jesus Christ our Lord. There are, then, two divinely constituted means: faith—the right kind of faith, in our Lord Jesus Christ—and obedience to His Word. Jesus said, "Ye believe in God, believe also in me" (John 14:1 KJV).

Faith in Jesus Christ, the right kind of faith, the only kind of faith that matters, is irrevocable, total commitment to the Person of Jesus Christ Himself. You cannot go back on it, and if it is total, there is nothing that is not included. Faith in Jesus is not gulping twice and saying, "I accept Jesus." It is getting into a state where you have totally committed yourself to the Lord Jesus Christ. It is irrevocable commitment to the Person of Jesus Christ.

Faith in Jesus is not commitment to your church or denomination. I believe in the local church; I am not a tabernacle man. I believe in the divine assembly. We ought to realize that we are, as a group of Christians, a divine assembly, a cell in the body of Christ, alive with His life. But not for one second would I try to create in you a faith that would lead you to commit yourself irrevocably to a local church or to your church leaders.

You are not asked to follow your church leaders. You are not asked like a little robin on the nest to open your innocent little mouth and just take anything I put in. If what I put in is not biblical food, regurgitate and do not be afraid to do it. Call me or come see me or write me an anonymous letter. But do something about it. Do not, by any means, swallow what your leaders give you. Here is the book, the Bible: go to it.

Faith is faith in Jesus Christ, God's Son. It is total faith in Christ and not in a denomination or church, though you may love the church and respect and love your leaders and your denomination. But your commitment is to Christ.

Obedience proves our love

Obedience to Christ proves we love Him, and in return He shows Himself to us. You say, "There are so many commandments, how can I obey? How can I remember them all, and can I be sure I am obeying?" In faith and love rest, wait and look. Then as His teaching touches your life, conform to it. There are some teachings of the Lord Jesus Christ that you would never get into because they would not touch you. They would not impinge on you in your present state. But as soon as they do touch you, then you automatically, sweetly and quietly obey.

A man was giving testimony about being

shipwrecked and praying, and about how the Lord delivered him. A dear old man of God went home, got on his knees and wept before the Lord. "God," he said, "You never saved me from shipwreck." And the Lord said, "Son, have you ever been at sea?" The man answered, "No." Of course you cannot save from shipwreck a man who has never been offshore. There are things that do not touch you, but the moment they do, obey instantly.

For instance, the Bible says, "Wives, submit to your husbands as to the Lord" (Ephesians 5:22). If you do not have any husband, why worry about that one? But if ever the words of our Lord Jesus Christ touch your life, instantly—because you are totally committed—gladly and quietly obey and do what you are told. He said that is your part, and His part is to manifest Himself to you and get you out of the rut.

Here are some examples from Luke.

Meanwhile, when a crowd of many thousands had gathered, so that they were trampling on one another, Jesus began to speak first to his disciples, saying: "Be on your guard against the yeast of the Pharisees, which is hypocrisy. There is nothing concealed that will not be disclosed, or hidden that will not be made known. What you have said in the dark will be heard in the daylight, and what you have whispered in the ear in the inner rooms will be proclaimed from the roofs. (12:1–3)

This teaches us that we are to be as candid and transparent as possible. There should be no secretiveness, no defensiveness, but openness and candidness. That is the teaching of Jesus. Instead of getting down on your knees and praying, "O Lord, get me these fish," catch some fish. Obey the Lord. Do what you are told. Use the constituted means. Be candid; put away that carefully cultured North American defensiveness. Don't be so afraid. You are not so bad. You do not have to be afraid to let people know who you are and what you are. Let down your hair, so to speak, and just be yourself.

Become children

The Lord said to become children. If we all became children, how beautiful that would be. You could walk up to a man and shake his hand without wondering, "Do I know enough judo to handle him?" He would not hurt you. Christians here are not going to hurt anybody, so just be perfectly candid. This is one passage you can practice no matter who you are or where you are. It touches you right now.

I tell you, whoever acknowledges me before men, the Son of Man will also ac-

knowledge him before the angels of God.
(12:8)

This passage tells us we are to testify and witness boldly about our Lord Jesus. If some of
you would begin to quietly witness where you
work, you would find a change coming over
you. "Whoever has my commands and obeys
them . . . [I will] show myself to him" (John
14:21).
You will get out of the rut when the Lord
begins to manifest Himself to you. But you
would rather go off somewhere and get down
on your knees and pray. Now praying is
right—I have taught and preached and prac-
ticed it since I was converted. But do not try to
pray down something that the Lord is telling
you to do. Do what you are told, and the Lord
will be right with you. Then instead of begging
you can praise.

> Then he said to them, "Watch out! Be on
> your guard against all kinds of greed; a
> man's life does not consist in the abun-
> dance of his possessions." (Luke 12:15)

Jesus gives the story of the man who was
covetous and lost his soul. So do not be
covetous—be generous. Do not be stingy, but
be free with your money. Do not be afraid—
thank the Lord, trust Him and put fear away.
These are examples of the constituted means of

faith and obedience. We sing this and do not know we are singing it: "Trust and obey, for there's no other way/ To be happy in Jesus, But to trust and obey." We sing that, but we have sung it so long that we might as well sing Mother Goose rhymes, because we do not know what we are singing.

Some of us are down in a spiritual rut, the old routine. Nothing has any taste to it. Some churches try to handle that by pandering to the situation, bringing in every kind of weird claptrap in order to get some of the poor half-dead people to get a little taste again.

We have God. We have Christ. We have truth. We have a world needing help. We have the saints, and we have the power of prayer. We have the joy of obedience and we have the sweet wonder of His presence. We have the joy of Christian song. We have all this and we do not need garbage. We have God. All we have to do is trust in His Son Jesus Christ and obey the truth, and the Lord will manifest Himself, show Himself through the lattice.

CHAPTER
6

Dealing with
Spiritual Problems

*I thank God, whom I serve, as my forefathers did,
with a clear conscience, as night and day I constantly remember you in my prayers. Recalling
your tears, I long to see you, so that I may be filled
with joy. I have been reminded of your sincere
faith, which first lived in your grandmother Lois
and in your mother Eunice and, I am persuaded,
now lives in you also. For this reason I remind you
to fan into flame the gift of God, which is in you
through the laying on of my hands. For God did
not give us a spirit of timidity, but a spirit of
power, of love and of self-discipline.*

*So do not be ashamed to testify about our Lord,
or ashamed of me his prisoner. But join with me in
suffering for the gospel, by the power of God. (2
Timothy 1:3–8)*

This passage contains a classic example of a
man who, if he was not already in the rut,
was in danger of getting into it. The old soldier,
Paul, was about to retire; that is, the Lord was
about to take him home. Before he went he

wrote a letter to his young coworker, much younger than he, but a noble young man. Timothy was full of faith, having been reared in a family where the faith of God was strong. He had proven himself a hundred ways in working with the great man Paul.

But even Timothy, though very busy and even because he was so busy, was in danger of settling into a rut. Otherwise Paul would not have said, "Fan the flame." In the King James this is translated "stir up the gift of God."

In Scripture God never uses superfluous words. He never says to a person who is wide awake, "Wake up!" He never says to a person who is lying down, "Lie down!" He never says to someone standing, "Get up!" And He never says to a person who is already stirred up, "Stir up!" God never wastes His words, and He never makes any little speeches like a person called upon at the laying of a cornerstone. Nor was Paul wasting words or giving a little talk that would be good just about anywhere. "Stir up the gift of God that is in thee"(KJV). Timothy needed this, or it would not have been written.

The evidence is that Timothy, even though a hard-working and faithful man, was in danger of getting into a rut. Paul said, in effect, "Don't be ashamed of the cross."

It is possible to be beaten until you are numb. You can smile and praise the Lord and say, "Jesus, I my cross have taken," for a while. But then you are slowly beaten until you are numb, and you get into a sort of a rut where you cannot fight back.

Timothy had been with Paul a long time, and Paul had been in so much trouble so much of the time. Timothy was tagging along behind in the same trouble, and Paul had noticed a little temptation to be ashamed of the cross. Essentially, Paul was saying, "Don't be ashamed of the cross. Don't shrink from the affliction of the gospel. God has not given us the spirit of fear." Then in Second Timothy 2:3 Paul said, "Endure hardship with us like a good soldier of Christ Jesus." It is as though he might have detected in the young man a little temptation to recoil a bit from the hard life he was called into.

Paul knew that Timothy was basically a sound man. He knew Timothy had been reared in a Christian home. He mentioned Timothy's grandmother, Lois, and his mother, Eunice. The grandmother and mother were both Christians, and good ones. Young Timothy had learned and become a Christian early in life. Paul knew that he was basically sound. But Paul was afraid that the pressure of things and the boredom of always being in the minority might put Timothy in danger of leveling off.

A personal revival

There is such a thing as a renaissance, a personal revival. The best illustration is the coming of the springtime on the farm. The snow will lay all winter long, and in some places you don't see the ground until springtime. How utterly dead everything looks, but you know that life is still there. The trees are stark, but there is life in them. The roots in the ground are all quiet, but there is life down there. Just below the frost line are the worms, the bugs, the mice, the moles and the chipmunks. They are all there, and there is life down there. They are all waiting for something, listening for Mother Nature to say, "Stir up the gift of God that is in thee."

Then comes the spring; the snow goes, and the blotches and patches begin to appear. The bobwhites begin to whistle their happy but monotonous song on the sunny side of the hill. The cattle begin to kick up their heels and run about the fields. That is spring. Pretty soon all the snow is gone, calves are born and lambs are about, and we start all over. Thank God, it is all new.

There is such a thing in the Christian life as going under for a winter. In other words, something happens to you, little by little, until you get snowed under and frozen over. There is life down there, covered up by the frost and ice. It may be hidden; it is there somewhere.

It is possible for us to go through spiritual experiences that can rouse us, the spiritual equivalent of a springtime in the meadow. I have seen it happen, and I would like to see it happen today.

The winter meadow illustration, as all illustrations, breaks down. The fields cannot be talked to. You have never heard of a farmer about February standing on a stump lecturing his fields. It is not done that way for this reason: these creatures have no moral perception and no wills of their own. They are dependent upon the position of the sun. They cannot do anything about their condition.

We have to enter in

But we can do something about ours. We can have the spiritual equivalent of springtime in the meadow, but we have to enter in. The tree waits it out, and even the animals have to wait it out. But you and I, being made in the image of God and having wills of our own, can do something about it. We can appeal directly to our hearts. We do not need to lie like a field covered over with snow. We can stir ourselves up. We can run to meet the sun. We can create our own crisis, because the job is not for meadow and grass, but for our own hearts. These other things only illustrate spiritual springtime. We can stir ourselves up. We can bring out the sun, and we can bring on the springtime.

How do we get this to happen? First it must come to the individual. I have no faith in anything that happens to a church that does not happen to the individual. If it does not affect the individual, numbers of individuals, if it is only a sort of social overtone that affects everybody momentarily, I have no faith in it at all.

David set the pattern for us. David confessed and repented. C.H. Spurgeon preached on repentance week after week, and somebody came to him and said, "When are you going to quit preaching on repentance, pastor?" Spurgeon replied, "When you repent." When we talk about confession and repentance, we keep right on talking about it until either it has had its effect or we know it will have none. To paraphrase the words of the Lord in such a situation, "Get the dust off your feet and hunt up someplace where they will listen." I have better hopes for you. I believe you will hear.

Charles Finney was a well-known preacher of the 19th century. Not all of us agree with everything that he taught, but we do believe that he was one of God's great men, perhaps one of the greatest evangelists who ever lived since the Apostle Paul. Finney said there were times or periods occasionally when he would get into a rut, and there would be a definite dimming of the power in his life. When that would happen, Finney said, "I took time off and waited on God in fasting and prayer until I was restored." That is the old-fashioned way of doing it, and that seems to be the way David did it. The Psalms were wet with David's salty tears as he confessed his sins to God, repented, took forgiveness and went his happy way.

The pad and pencil method

Try what I call the pad and pencil method. This method is very simple and consists of getting on your knees with your Bible, a pad of paper and a pencil. Read the Bible and then write down what is wrong with you. The only way to remain spiritual is to keep after yourself. The pad and pencil method is good. Read, for example, the Sermon on the Mount. When the Holy Spirit says, "You are that person," write it down. Read on. When the Holy Spirit says you are wrong here or there, write it down. Then set your Bible aside and go over your list before God in confession with the promise that you will never be caught doing those things again. Commune with your own heart, be still and question yourself like a doctor with your open Bible before you.

You will find that this will bring sunshine to your life, and you will have springtime in your heart. When you get before God realizing that there has been a bit of snow on the ground and that the happy song of the birds is not heard in the land and that the sweet smell of the flowers is not within you, begin to question yourself before God with the open Bible. The symptoms you already know, but try to get at the causes. If you are evasive with God, then there will be no help. If you are evasive with yourself, if you rationalize your weaknesses, you will get no help.

Ask some questions

Here are some questions I recommend you ask yourself. In quiet silence ask, "Am I always truthful and honest? I claim to be a Christian, and I believe that the root of the matter is in me and the seed of God is in my heart. I believe I am the Lord's child, but I am not satisfied with the frozen-over rut. Lord, help me to be honest while I answer. Am I always truthful on the telephone? Am I always honest with my creditors, with my employers, with my employees and in all social contracts and contacts?"

Somebody may say, "What's the difference?" Dishonesty and shading of the truth are sins that grieve the Holy Spirit and bring on the winter. The winter of your discontent may be upon you, and like the life in a leafless tree, your life is buried within. You may have grieved the Holy Spirit by untruthfulness. One of the first things Christians have to do is become perfectly honest with God and perfectly truthful in everything they say.

Another question to put to yourself is, "Do I have any habits I am ashamed to let anybody know I have? Have I any personal habits that I am ashamed of? Do I hide something when the pastor is coming? If everything were known in the church about how I lived, would I go back to church?" You can dodge this, twist it around and answer evasively, but the snow will lie on your heart. If you answer God honestly and go to work to get rid of it and clean it up, springtime will come for you.

Then ask yourself, "Is my speech clean?" One of the most shocking things in the church is the dirty-mouthed Christian who always walks on the borderline. There is no place for borderline stories that embarrass some people, and there is nothing about sex or the human body that is funny if your mind is clean.

There was once a gathering of officers, and George Washington was present in the room. One of the young officers began to think about a dirty story that he wanted to tell, and he got a smirk on his face. He looked around and said, "I'm thinking of a story. I guess there are no ladies present." Washington straightened up and said, "No, young man, but there are gentlemen." The young officer shut his mouth and kept the dirty story inside his dirty head and heart.

Anything you could not tell with Jesus present, do not tell. Anything you could not laugh at were Jesus present, do not laugh at.

Ask yourself another question. "Am I using my money wisely? Am I using my money to bless people? Am I using my money to help find the lost sheep? Am I using my money to help feed the hungry children?"

Here is yet another question: "Do I gossip about people? Have I been a troublemaker?" Some people are disease carriers who are not sick themselves. They carry some disease, but they are not ill—just carriers. There are some Christians who are carriers. They can say "amen" with the best and can sing "Nearer My God to Thee" with the loudest, but they are not around very long until suspicions begin to enter the minds of Christians. They are troublemakers and trouble carriers.

Then, "Have I judged other Christians?" Your present frozen condition may be a judgment of God, for as you judge others so you will be judged by God. Your present frozen condition may be that you have judged somebody else to be frozen, and the Lord allowed the thing to turn around on you.

"Am I heavenly minded or earthly minded? Where do my thoughts tend to stray when they are free to stray where they will? What do I brood over? Are my thoughts pure and charitable?" If you can find out what you brood over, you will know what kind of a Christian you are and what kind of a heart you have. We always brood over things that we love, or that we hate if we are holding a grudge against somebody.

"Am I faithful in prayer?" Ask yourself that. "Well, I'm busy," you say. Yes, you are busy. So was the Lord Jesus. So was Martin Luther. Luther said, "In the morning I have so much work to do that I am going to have to pray longer today." Are you faithful in prayer, and do you meditate on the Word? How much of

Scripture have you read lately? Have you read it with meditation and tenderness?

These are a few questions. You can answer them evasively and the snow lies there. Or you can answer them honestly and see the springtime come to your heart.

Put yourself in the hands of the One who loves you infinitely. If you have failed Him, you will have to admit that there is a rut or snow on the meadow. Tell Him so—don't hide it. He will not turn His back in anger and say, "You disappointed me and betrayed me." There is a balm in Gilead, plenty of it. The balm and healing in the blood of the Lamb will get you out of the rut.

Three Spiritual Laws

Therefore, I urge you, brothers, in view of God's mercy, to offer your bodies as living sacrifices, holy and pleasing to God—this is your spiritual act of worship. Do not conform any longer to the pattern of this world, but be transformed by the renewing of your mind. Then you will be able to test and approve what God's will is—his good, pleasing and perfect will. (Romans 12:1–2)

The Bible says that we are to present our bodies "as living sacrifices, holy and pleasing to God." Of course, if you give your body, you give everything it contains. That means giving yourself wholly to God, and the idea of giving yourself wholly to God contains three laws.

The first law is the law of *surrender*. If you do not surrender, it will be totally impossible for the Lord to do anything for you. Surgeons have to have the surrender of their patients. If I went to a surgeon and insisted that I was going to tell him how to do the job and not only that but stay awake and resist him, the surgeon could not work. It would be impossible. Surgeons must put their patients to sleep so they cannot resist, so they are in a state of surrender. That is the law of surrender.

A more beautiful and biblical description is the story of the potter and the clay, which illustrates the law of surrender further. The potter has soft, yielding clay, but if the clay does not surrender, the potter cannot do a thing with it. If there are burnt places, hard places or unsurrendered places in the clay, though the potter be a genius in making vessels, the artist still could not make anything useful and beautiful out of an unyielding blob of clay. It is possible for an object to be useful but not beautiful, like a garbage can. It is also entirely possible to be beautiful and not useful, like the lily. The lily has no utilitarian place in the world.

It is possible to have a vessel that is useful without being beautiful. The old cream crocks in our spring house on the farm were useful all right. You could pour the milk in them, wait for the cream to rise and skim it off. They were not beautiful, but they were quite useful. Everybody has in their home beautiful little knickknacks. They are utterly useless, simply to be enjoyed for their beauty. But God wants His vessels to be both useful and beautiful. If God is going to make those kinds of vessels out of us, however, we are going to have to yield to the law of surrender. Give yourself to God as a living sacrifice and let Him have you—all of you.

The law of concentration

Then there is the law of *concentration*. The secret of every successful person is concentration. Take a musician, for example. Most musicians are mediocre because they do not have time to concentrate. They might have greater ability than they are ever able to bring out because other things take their time. But an excellent musician must study and practice five and six hours a day. They must give themselves to it completely and concentrate.

Consider an athlete. The average person goes on the church picnic and plays softball or tosses horseshoes once or twice a year. That is not an athlete.

Athletes are people who live for sports all the time. They play with their teams during the season, and off season they hunt and fish, hustle about, take long hikes and keep themselves in shape. They always have to remember those arms, those hands, those biceps. They are always exercising. They could never say, "Give me two more helpings of pie with whipped cream," or, "I'm going to sleep for a couple days." They could never do that—their main concern would be to keep those muscles in shape. That is the law of concentration. Athletes have to concentrate on what they are doing. If they do not, they will only be mediocre sandlot athletes.

It is the same with scientists. Sometimes people have thought that scientists were a bit off because they gave themselves wholly to their research. Thomas Edison slept only four hours a night, since he was so totally given to his research and projects. He lived for nothing else. The result was that he managed to produce many important inventions. That is the law of concentration.

Musicians, athletes and scientists may do other things, but they have just one thing to which they are totally committed.

The law of fascination

Third, there is the law of *fascination*. This is a little harder to understand, but it is just as real. To be fascinated, according to the dictionary, is to be held spellbound by some irresistible charm. If something does not fascinate us, we can take it or leave it. It is like the various art exhibitions. I can take them or leave them. Some people think a lot of the exhibitions, and I will go if somebody invites me; but I am not fascinated by them. I am not drawn to them by a charm that I cannot break. But in the kingdom of God there is the law of fascination, the law of irresistible charm. Christians who do not know the law will never be anything but half-Christians all their lives. They will always be in the rut.

The law of fascination as seen in the world is often a personal tragedy. Being fascinated by something evil, base or unworthy can be a terrible tragedy.

For example, some young girls may be determined that they are going to be movie stars. They start at 13 to pluck out their eyebrows and paint themselves up and stand in front of those tall mirrors trying to look like Jayne Mansfield. I suppose all girls go through a phase sometime where they want to be something they will never be, and we will not be too hard on them. But if they do not get over it, and if they begin to want it so badly they sell themselves for it, they may concentrate on it to a point where they are so fascinated by it, their fascination leads them to dismiss their parents as old fogies. They leave home, as many do, and go to the big city to try to make good, determined that they will see their names out in front of the theater. That can be a great curse.

Many men want to be rich. The average businessman wants to make enough money to keep his family comfortable and to have a little left for a rainy day. We can understand that desire. John Wesley used to say, "Make all you can so you can give away all you can." Wesley wanted his people to work hard and make a lot of money so they could use it for the Lord's work. That may be a pardonable reason for making as much as possible. But there have been men who have become so enamored of gold that they sold themselves out on the market, sold their hearts and souls in order that they might be rich.

The most pitiful creature in the world is the gambler. The gambler is enamored of gambling, utterly fascinated by it. Fascination can lead to a person's inability to escape, caught by the wicked charm that evil things have.

Our Lord turns it around and says, "Come to me, all you who are weary and burdened. . . . Take my yoke upon you and learn from me, for I am gentle and humble in heart, and you will find rest for your souls" (Matthew 11:28–29). In effect He says, "Come to me and be fascinated by me. Concentrate upon me, surrender to me, and yield so completely to me that you can give all to me."

Who has a right to say this? Who has the right to talk like this? Those who knew Him best try to tell us. I suppose they have not succeeded very well, even though the Scriptures are inspired. I am quite sure they do not tell us all that can be known about God. They only tell us as much as they can. Because those inspired men were human and those to whom they wrote were human, there was imperfection and limitation in both the inspired ones and those who read the inspired words. God was not able to say all that He could say about Himself. I am sure the archangels that burn before the throne of God could tell us more about God than we know, even though we have an inspired Bible to tell us. Nevertheless, those who knew Him best tried to tell us.

Moses took us back to the beginning of all that we see, all that we call the universe. He took us back before the stars and moon were, before space was and before time was, and said, "In the beginning God created the heavens and the earth" (Genesis 1:1). So Moses said that the One who calls us to Himself has a right to do so because He antedates time, He transcends space, He fills His universe and He is God.

The psalmist also wrote what he knew.

Praise the LORD, O my soul.

O LORD my God, you are very great;
    you are clothed with splendor and
        majesty.
He wraps himself in light as with a
        garment;
    he stretches out the heavens like a
        tent
    and lays the beams of his upper
        chambers on their waters.
He makes the clouds his chariot
    and rides on the wings of the wind.
He makes winds his messengers,
    flames of fire his servants.

He set the earth on its foundations;

it can never be moved.
You covered it with the deep as with a
    garment. (Psalm 104:1–6a)

David, in Psalm 103, showed that this God is
not only a God who makes mountains, hills,
rivers and streams, who rides upon the wings
of the clouds, but He loves His people. "For as
high as the heavens are above the earth, so
great is his love for those who fear him" (v. 11).
"But from everlasting to everlasting the Lord's
love is with those who fear him, and his
righteousness with their children's children—
with those who keep his covenant and remember to obey his precepts" (vv. 17–18). David
tried to impart the incommunicable, tried to
tell what cannot be told of the wonder of God.
    Isaiah asked who could compare with God.

Who has measured the waters in the
    hollow of his hand,
  or with the breadth of his hand
    marked off the heavens?
Who has held the dust of the earth in a
    basket,
  or weighed the mountains on the scales
  and the hills in a balance?
Who has understood the mind of the
    LORD,
  or instructed him as his counselor?
Whom did the LORD consult to
    enlighten him,

and who taught him the right way?
Who was it that taught him knowledge
or showed him the path of
    understanding? (Isaiah 40:12–14)

In the New Testament, John tried to tell us about God. "In the beginning was the Word, and the Word was with God, and the Word was God" (1:1). "The Word became flesh and made his dwelling among us. We have seen his glory, the glory of the One and Only, who came from the Father, full of grace and truth" (1:14). John the Mystic tried to tell us how great God is.

The Apostle Paul also gave us insight on who God is.

> For in Christ all the fullness of the Deity lives in bodily form, and you have been given fullness in Christ, who is the head over every power and authority. (Colossians 2:9–10)

> And having disarmed the powers and authorities, he made a public spectacle of them, triumphing over them by the cross.
> Therefore do not let anyone judge you by what you eat or drink, or with regard to a religious festival, a New Moon celebration or a Sabbath day. These are a shadow of the things that were to come; the reality, however, is found in Christ. (2:15–17)

Why am I giving you all these passages of Scripture? Because I want to tell you who it is who says, "Present your bodies to me. Take your cross and follow me. Give yourself wholly to me. Surrender to me. Concentrate upon me and learn to be fascinated by me." He is the only One who can say it.

There is only one Man whom we can trust to follow. That Man is Jesus Christ. Why is He different from any other person? Why do I refuse to follow other people, and yet follow this Man? Of no other person can it be said, "In the beginning was the Word, and the Word was with God, and the Word was God" (John 1:1). "The Word became flesh and made his dwelling among us. We have seen his glory, the glory of the One and Only, who came from the Father, full of grace and truth" (1:14). Of no other person from Adam to now can it be said, "He will be called Wonderful Counselor, Mighty God, Everlasting Father, Prince of Peace" (Isaiah 9:6). Of no one else can it be said that three days after He had gone into the grave He rose again. Of no other person can it be said that while they beheld Him,

. . . he was taken up before their very eyes, and a cloud hid him from their sight.

They were looking intently up into the sky as he was going, when suddenly two men dressed in white stood beside them. "Men of Galilee," they said, "why do you stand here looking into the sky? This same Jesus, who has been taken from you into heaven, will come back in the same way you have seen him go into heaven."(Acts 1:9–11)

Of none other can it be said,

There . . . was a white horse, whose rider is called Faithful and True. With justice he judges and makes war. His eyes are like blazing fire, and on his head are many crowns. He has a name written on him that no one knows but he himself. He is dressed in a robe dipped in blood, and his name is the Word of God. (Revelation 19:11–13)

This is the King of glory, this Man; and this Man is the one who says, "Give yourself to me. Surrender to me and concentrate upon me. Be caught in the spell of the irresistible charm."

If we do not feel this, we do not have to be argued into it. Jacob was a rascal, and yet God blessed him; Esau was apparently a good fellow, and God did not bless him. What was the difference?

One had the fascination. He felt the law of fascination within his heart. He needed a lot of help, and he was anything but a good man to start with, but something in his heart was leaping up. Deep was calling unto deep, and deep was responding unto deep. The voice of the little man was responding to the voice of the great God. That is why Jacob became Israel, following the work of grace that transformed him from his carnal state into his blessed state of spirituality.

If you do not have this fascination, it could be that you are but another Esau. What a tragedy to be born of the red clay and live and die and be buried in the red clay. Shakespeare said of Caesar, "That though he be the emperor yet give nature time and nature will reduce him to a bit of clay that might be used to keep the wind away." The great Persian poet Omar Khayyam said, "When you drink out of that vessel, drink reverently; it may be your grandfather's dust out of which it is made."

What a tragedy to be born out of the red clay and live a secular, earthly life and then die and be buried out of sight in that same red clay. But if you feel the charm, the tug and the pull of God, you will know what the Holy Spirit meant when He said, "I urge you, brothers, in view of God's mercy, to offer your bodies as living sacrifices, holy and pleasing to God— this is your spiritual act of worship" (Romans 12:1).

How do you get out of the religious rut? You get out of the rut by giving God your all, letting God have you completely. Concentrate your whole life on God and His Son Jesus Christ. Then seek to know the sweet fascination of loving God. You cannot stay asleep very long when the beauty of Jesus is before your eyes. Some have been asleep long enough. If you could only wake to the voice of your Beloved. If you could only be awakened and roused and hear Him speak, it would be sweeter than the voice of the mocking bird, sweeter than the sound of the harp. The voice of God's Son—that would get you out of the rut, and that would get you out of your sleep. Jesus Christ is God's music, God's poetry, God's art, God's beauty, God's all.

Breaking
the Status Quo

*The LORD our God said to us at Horeb, "You have
stayed long enough at this mountain. Break camp
and advance into the hill country of the Amorites;
go to all the neighboring peoples in the Arabah, in
the mountains, in the western foothills, in the
Negev and along the coast, to the land of the
Canaanites and to Lebanon, as far as the great
river, the Euphrates. See, I have given you this
land. Go in and take possession of the land that the
LORD swore he would give to your fathers—to
Abraham, Isaac and Jacob—and to their descendants after them." (Deuteronomy 1:6–8)*

Israel allowed themselves to settle down and
became contented with circumstances that
were all right, but which could and did break
their spirit of adventure and cause them to accept the status quo as being final for them.
Every once in a while through prophet, apostle
or psalmist, God stretches out His hand and
tries to arouse His people from their sleep.

Somebody once said that man is made of dust and dust tends to settle. People tend to settle down and do the same things year in and year out, slowly going around in a circle. When this gets into religion, it is deadly and evil.

The majority of Christians are asleep and in a spiritual rut. Sometimes Christians who realize they are in a rut put pressure on others to adopt their viewpoint. But even if truth does not convince and persuade a man or woman, nobody has the right to set up a psychological squeeze on someone else. If people yield under pressure, it shows that they are too weak to resist. If they are too weak to resist, and if they take a religious position because they are too weak to resist, they will also be too weak to persist. When we follow Christ there must be persistence. We must go on.

To apply pressure, a person projects himself or herself into the minds and consciences of people made in the image of God and forces them psychologically to do something they have no particular reason for wanting to do. They are not basically interested in it and have no satisfactory reason for doing it, but they are under pressure. If they do not have a reason for doing what they are going to do, they will not know why they are involved. Then when they get out they will not be sure that they were in, and so the whole process makes for weak, spineless religion. This violates the law of human nature, which dictates that all valid acts must arise from a natural urge or from a convinced mind.

An example of a natural urge is when you are hungry. You may be very hungry, but your hunger does not have a high intellectual content in it. Nobody needs to stand up and say, "Now, all you who are hungry raise your hands." You know you are hungry, and you just go out to eat. Hunger is a natural urge.

Another legitimate reason for an act is a convinced mind. I am convinced that I ought to do something, and I do it because I have a conviction that it ought to be done.

Those are the only two reasons for doing anything. If I force people under psychological pressure and steamroll them into doing something because they are too weak to resist, I have violated their nature. Our approach to getting people out of the rut, then, must not be to pressure them to do something they don't want to do. Instead, we must present the truth and let the Holy Spirit prompt them to want to escape.

Must get out of rut

It is imperative not only that we Christians get out of our rut but that we get out *now*. You know if you are in. If you are not getting any prayers answered, or if your prayers are so vague you are not sure but what any answer might have been an accident, you are in the rut. If you are living far from God, yet hoping you are saved, you are in the rut. If you are not progressing, if you are where you were months or years ago, if you have settled down and learned to live with yourself and adjusted to your present spiritual state, you are in the rut.

There are some reasons why it is imperative that we as a church and as individuals get out, and get moving on our way to a better spiritual life. One is that you have not much time to do anything about it. Your own interest is going to flag before long. Change is absolutely imperative to getting out of the rut, but the older we get the less we feel the need to change. If people have an urge within their spirits based upon a belief and conviction that they ought to move—to begin to reassess their lives and adjust their living—then they ought to do it right now while they are thinking about it.

Another reason for getting out of the rut now is the danger of political developments that will make it less favorable to serve God. In human history there have never been two countries like the United States and Canada—not even England—where it was more favorable to become a Christian. But the political situation could easily shift around so the climate is not so favorable. There are many countries where the political and social climate is not favorable to becoming a Christian. Anybody who wants to become a Christian in some countries of the world has a rough time of it. But here the people help you along.

Could you afford to wait until the climate shifted so it were not so favorable, until the social situation shifted so it were not so favorable? If you have not taken advantage of this favorable climate to get right with God and to improve your spiritual life in this freedom, would you if you were forbidden?

The Lord may soon return

The next reason is that the Lord may soon return. I realize there is a lot that we do not know about prophecy, but most Christians are looking for the second coming of the Lord. They expect Him to come. They do not know when He will come, and the ones who claim they do, do not. Nevertheless, He may come in your lifetime. He said that He would come back in an hour when we think not. It could be that this present decline in expectation may have an ominous significance. It can easily be said that this would be the time when fewer people are expecting the Lord. Thirty years ago everybody was expecting the Lord and talking about it. Now few are thinking and less are talking about it. If you press people, they will admit that they believe in the second coming of Christ, but they are not looking for it expectantly.

The last thing that bears upon the imperativeness of doing something about our spiritual life now is that we have such a short time to prepare for such a long time. By that I mean we have now to prepare for then. We have an hour to prepare for eternity. To fail to prepare is an act of moral folly. For anyone to have a day given to prepare, it is an act of inexcusable folly to let anything hinder that preparation. If we find ourselves in a spiritual rut, nothing in the world should hinder us. Nothing in this world is worth it. If we believe in eternity, if we believe in God, if we believe in the eternal existence of the soul, then there is nothing important enough to cause us to commit such an act of moral folly.

Failing to get ready in time for eternity, and failing to get ready now for the great then that lies out yonder, is a trap in plain sight. There is an odd saying in the Old Testament, "How useless to spread a net in full view of all the birds" (Proverbs 1:17). When the man of God wrote that, he gave the birds a little credit. It would be silly for a bird watching me set the trap to conveniently fly down and get into it. Yet there are people doing that all the time. People who have to live for eternity fall into that trap set for them in plain sight.

It is folly to put off to a tomorrow because you may never see the things that you should do now. It is an act of inexcusable folly to count on help that will never come. It is foolish to ignore God's help now offered us. Many are guilty of ignoring the help that is presently being extended to them, all the while waiting for help that will never come from others.

There is not much that can be said in favor of lazy or careless Christians. God never told anyone to do anything that he or she could not do. Jesus said to the man with the paralyzed arm that hung at his side like a limp piece of flesh, "Stretch out your hand" (Matthew 12:13a). And the man, believing that Jesus was the Christ, stretched out his hand and was healed instantly. God has never asked anyone yet to do anything that He was not enabling the person to do.

CHAPTER
9

The Voice
of God Speaking

This message is born out of three things: the Word of God, the Holy Spirit and the present religious situation. If it is not born out of the Word of God, then I want nothing to do with it whatever. But it is also born out of the Holy Spirit—it is the burden, the grief and the joy of the Holy Spirit.

I would say to you who are wondering about the Spirit-filled life: If you just want to be happy, and nothing else, you had better steer away from the Spirit-filled life. The same Holy Spirit who will give you joy will also allow you to share His burdens and griefs. Out of the burden, grief, joy and victory of the Holy Spirit come these messages.

God's Word says that a faithful and wise steward gives the people their meat in due season. Some people preach the Bible all right, and you cannot deny that. But they go to the Bible as you would to a medical book to find out what you should prescribe. But instead of prescribing to suit each patient, they just prescribe for everybody at one time.

When a preacher is not preaching to a given situation, it is like giving medicine to people indiscriminately. That approach is not particularly fitted for teaching the Word of God. Even though it may be faithful and true, without any regard to the current situation, it is like teaching the multiplication table.

The New Testament epistles were written to specific conditions, as were the seven letters of Revelation. Particular situations developed, and then the man of God wrote to these particular people. The seven letters found in Revelation were to particular churches, having regard to the needs of those churches.

It was the same with the prophets of the Old Testament. No prophet went into an ivory tower, settled down to relax, read deeply awhile, took out a pen and said, "Now, I'm going to write a book of prophecy." They did not do it that way. They wrote to the need, to the situation. They aimed their arrows at a target. When God is speaking to a particular situation the power of the Holy Spirit is present and active.

When David sinned, Nathan the prophet came to him and told a little parable. When David gave his judgment of what to do with the sinful man, Nathan pointed his finger at the king and said, "You are the man" (2 Samuel 12:7a). Immediately David threw off his crown

and his robe, dropped his scepter, fell on his
knees and repented before God. That was a
particular situation. When we are talking to a
specific situation the sheep are separated from
the goats, the veil is removed and the judgment
begins.

The question is not, "Is this the voice of God
to us?" I hope nobody will try to evade responsibility that way. There are two other questions
before us. The first question is: How many of
us are willing to hear the voice of God? Jesus
said,

> Therefore I am sending you prophets and
> wise men and teachers. Some of them you
> will kill and crucify; others you will flog in
> your synagogues and pursue from town to
> town.
> O Jerusalem, Jerusalem, you who kill the
> prophets and stone those sent to you, how
> often I have longed to gather your children
> together, as a hen gathers her chicks under
> her wings, but you were not willing. Look,
> your house is left to you desolate. (Mat-
> thew 23:34, 37–38)

Were these people willing to hear the voice of
God? Thousands of years before Christ was
born in Bethlehem, the Holy Spirit said,

> Wisdom calls aloud in the street,
> she raises her voice in the public squares;

at the head of the noisy streets she
    cries out,
  in the gateways of the city she
    makes her speech:
"How long will you simple ones love
    your simple ways?
How long will mockers delight in
    mockery
and fools hate knowledge?
If you had responded to my rebuke,
  I would have poured out my heart to
    you
and made my thoughts known to you.
But since you rejected me when I called
  and no one gave heed when I
    stretched out my hand,
since you ignored all my advice
and would not accept my rebuke,
I in turn will laugh at your disaster;
  I will mock when calamity overtakes
    you." (Proverbs 1:20–26)

The second question is: How many are worthy to hear His voice? In Acts 13:46b Paul and
Barnabas told the people, "Since you reject it . .
. . we now turn to the Gentiles." This is a terrible judgment. But here is the gist of what I
want to say: A radical and sweeping reformation is imperative among the people called
Christians—Protestants generally and evangelicals in particular.

What is meant by reformation? Some may

recoil from that word; I have heard people say, "I do not believe in reformation—I believe in regeneration." That sounds good and it gets some amens, but the fact is, if you do not have reformation you cannot have regeneration. The Holy Spirit will not come and regenerate carnal, stubborn people who will not obey Him.

First there must be a reformation.

> Wash and make yourselves clean.
> Take your evil deeds
>   out of my sight!
> Stop doing wrong,
>   learn to do right!
> Seek justice,
>   encourage the oppressed.
> Defend the cause of the fatherless,
>   plead the case of the widow.
> "Come now, let us reason together,"
>   says the LORD.
> "Though your sins are like scarlet,
>   they shall be as white as snow;
> though they are red as crimson,
>   they shall be like wool."
>   (Isaiah 1:16–18)

Sweeping reformation

We need sweeping reformation. Let me give a definition of reformation as it is given in a religious dictionary: "Change by removal of faults or abuses, and a restoration to a former good estate." Now that is not so bad. I do not know how anybody who believes he or she is a Christian could ever object to changing in the direction of the removal of faults and abuses toward the restoration to a former good estate.

The problem is change, which disturbs many people. They have accepted the status quo as being the very tablets given by God on the mountain. Most people, if they happen to be in any church anywhere, accept the status quo without knowing or caring to inquire how it came to be. In other words, they do not ask, "Oh God, is this of You, is this divine, is this out of the Bible?" Because it was done and is being done, and because a lot of people are doing it, they assume it is all right.

Then songs are written about it, and it gets into magazines. Pretty soon people are called to it, and the first thing we know we have gotten into a religious situation that is not of God. It is not according to Scripture, and God is not pleased with it at all. Rather, He is angry. Yet we do not know it because we do not like the word *change*. The change took place slowly, before we arrived on the scene, and we think because it is everywhere it is therefore right. We accept the status quo, the existing state of affairs, and say, "This is it," forgetting that history demonstrates that religions invariably degenerate.

This is hard for people to face up to. Religion deteriorates just as fruit rots and just as people get old in spite of all they try to do at the drug stores. It is inevitable that we get old, and so it is with religion. It is built-in that we start to deteriorate shortly after God comes and blesses us.

Look what happened to Israel. God called Israel out of Egypt, and it began to deteriorate before it reached the Red Sea. Then He gave it a revival by taking it through the Red Sea and into the wilderness. But Israel started to degenerate before it had gone 20 miles in the wilderness. As a result the people eventually wandered for 40 years.

You can follow the history of Israel and see the story of the kings. It is a depressing story. Here is a man. He lived and did evil in the sight of the Lord. He had a son, and his son did evil in the sight of the Lord as his father before him. The status quo was maintained.

Dare to question status quo

Today we need people who dare to question the status quo and say, "Wait a minute here. Where do you find this in the Bible?" The idea that all you have to do is to accept Christ and you are in is a great mistake. It leaves people with the impression that if they accept Christ they have no fight to fight, no warfare, no job to do and no temptations. They are just in. When you accept Christ rightly as your Lord and Savior you are in, but to be honest, you have just started to fight.

People get converted and we do not tell them

that they must fight all the way through to heaven because of the spirit of degeneration and the tendency to deteriorate. They must fight, pray through, suffer it out and live in praise and worship, because if they do not they will deteriorate. Read the history of the Christian church if you can keep your faith and keep from weeping.

Then there is the removal of faults and abuses. Where are the faults and abuses? Look around at the religious scene and you will see the faults, the abuses and the desperate need for change.

Where are the model saints? We ought to be raising model saints, the kind Christians could take as examples and say, "I want to follow these men and women and be like them as they are like their Lord." But we are simply not producing saints in this generation. Most Christians are bad examples to other Christians. We work hard to get people converted, and we think we do God's service. Then after we get them converted and they get to know us, we are bad examples to them. I consider this an abuse in the church of Christ.

If we evangelicals had one-third of the enthusiasm of some of the cults we could take a continent. We have the power and they do not—that is, we have power available to us and they do not. We have a lazy bunch of evangelicals on our hands.

Another fault is carnality. The Apostle Paul

talked about the carnal Christians of Corinth, and he labored and prayed and wept over the carnality of those Christians. This describes most evangelicals today: carnal, immature, without miracles, without wonders, lacking a wonderful sense of the presence of the Lord, held together by social activities and nothing else.

Another roadblock to reformation is prayerlessness among God's people. For 100 years the Moravians never stopped praying. They staffed a prayer tower as a factory staffs its machines. In eight-hour shifts the Moravians continued their prayer vigil for 100 years.

Carelessness is another fault among evangelicals. Careless Christians do not discipline or examine themselves. Plato once said, "A life that is not examined is a kind of death." People who simply live by their instincts and do the best they can, but do not examine themselves are careless and, according to Plato, may as well be dead.

Then there is coldness of heart. The temperature of many evangelical churches is so chilly that nobody imagines that he or she is cold in the heart. We sing songs that were written out of hearts that were hot as fire. We sing them coldly to a creeping tempo.

That is evangelicalism as we have it today throughout the continent. It costs a lot for the rattles for the saints, for the teething rings for the children of the Most High.

An Unchanging Book
in an Ever-changing
World

*So he said to me, "This is the word of the LORD
to Zerubbabel: 'Not by might nor by power, but by
my Spirit,' says the LORD Almighty." (Zechariah
4:6)*

One area of thinking that needs reform is
our practical beliefs about God's design
for mankind. I emphasize *practical* beliefs, because there is a difference between nominal
beliefs and practical ones. A nominal belief is
what you hold in name, and the practical belief
is what you hold in reality and what holds you.
While probably there are not many faults to be
found with the nominal beliefs, there are a
great deal to be found with the practical beliefs.
These practical beliefs need restoration to their
happy and bright state with faults and abuses
purged.

It has been a long time since Jesus was born
in Bethlehem, died on the cross, rose again the

third day, ascended to the right hand of God
the Father Almighty and sent the Holy Spirit to
establish His church. Since those days there
have been changes in the world so radical,
sweeping, all-pervading and revolutionary as
to be entirely incredible to anybody living in
Jesus' day.

Restoration to belief in the truth

Today's world was entirely unimaginable to
the people of those times. Have these changes
forced God to modify His plans for His church
and for mankind? Here is where we have fallen
by the wayside. Here is where we need a reformation, a purgation, a removal of the faults
and a restoration again of the faith of Christians to a belief in the truth.

Many Christians say, without a question,
"Yes, that is true." Actually, I suppose they
would not like to have it put to them like that:
People do not like the most realistic construc-
tions. What would the liberals and modernists
say if you backed them in a corner with the
question, "Do you think God has been forced
to change His mind?" I do not think anybody
would quite have the courage to say yes.
Nevertheless, they do say it little by little until
they have brainwashed their people.

In effect, they say that the Bible must be interpreted in the light of new developments. A
book that was written in the day when people
rode donkeys must be reinterpreted to mesh

with contemporary society. They say that the prophets and apostles mistook what God intended to do. The Bible is outmoded and largely irrelevant. *Irrelevant* means that it is not related to anything. *Outmoded* means we have new modes of thinking and living now, so the Bible is out-of-date—a back-issue magazine. We must, therefore, reassess its teachings and rethink our beliefs and hopes.

I am not overstating this at all. This is what is being taught today. It gets into the newspapers, and people are saying that the Bible must be interpreted in the light of all these changes. The apostles and prophets were mistaken. They had ideas that were good and advanced for their day, but not advanced for our day. We know more about ourselves, human motivation and the nature of things than they did back then. Therefore a book written when people thought the earth was flat and the sun rose in the morning, crossed over the earth and went down into the sea cannot possibly be taken seriously. While it certainly contains some beautiful poetry and some marvelously inspiring thoughts about human nature and the world in which we live, nevertheless all this is to be understood and reinterpreted, reassessed and rethought.

I challenge the idea that we are advanced. I know the majority of modern educators, newspaper writers, TV personalities, radio reporters, politicians and all the rest do not agree with me. Nevertheless, I challenge the idea that we are any further advanced than they were in the days of Jesus.

If we are so advanced, then I want to ask some questions. Why do we kill thousands of human beings each year with automobiles? Because we ride automobiles instead of donkeys, we are advanced? If we are so advanced in our day, why are the penitentiaries packed full and the mental hospitals crowded? If we are so advanced, why is the whole world a powder keg? If we are so advanced, how is it that we have weapons that can annihilate the world? If we are so advanced, why is it that people cannot walk alone in the parks anymore? Why is it that workers who get out at midnight never walk home alone anymore? Why is it in this advanced age that drugs, violence, abortion and divorce are soaring?

There is a mind-set that thinks every motion is progress. Every time you move you are progressing. Then there is the mind-set that thinks whenever you move in a straight line you are going forward, forgetting that you can move in a straight line and be going backward.

The tragedy of the century

The tragedy of the century is that Protestants have accepted this as progress and actually believe it. The children of the protesters, children of the Reformation, have been brainwashed and indoctrinated by those who believe that changes have made a difference in God's plan, a difference in Christianity and a difference in Christ. We have been brainwashed to believe that we cannot read the Bible as we used to. We must now read it through glasses colored by change. We have been hypnotized by the serpent, the devil, into believing that we no longer have a trustworthy Bible, so Protestantism is no longer a moral force in the world.

Protestantism is not a force in this world because we have sold out to the brainwashers. Instead of being the sons and daughters of the protesters, we are now yes-men and yes-women. Running our Protestant world are people who talk solemnly about Christ but who do not mean what the Bible means. They talk about revelation and inspiration, but they do not mean what our fathers meant.

The second prominent tragedy is that the gospel churches are confused and intimidated by numbers. They accept the belief that there has been change and that Christians must adjust to the change. The word used is *adjustment*. We must get adjusted, forgetting that the world has always been blessed by the people who were not adjusted. The poor people who get adjusted cannot do much anyhow. They are not worth having around.

In every field of human endeavor progress has been made by those who stood up and said, "I will not adjust to the world." The classical composers, poets and architects were people who would not adjust. Today society insists that if you do not adjust you will get a complex. If you do not get adjusted, you will have to go to a psychiatrist.

Jesus was maladjusted

Jesus was among the most maladjusted people in His generation. He never pretended to adjust to the world. He came to die for the world and to call the world to Himself, and the adjustment had to be on the other side.

The contemporary world is a result of radical changes down the generations amounting to revolution: the scientific revolution, the industrial revolution, the communications revolution, the philosophical revolution and the social revolution. Are we going to accept the belief that the Bible must be interpreted anew in the light of these developments? Are we going to allow ourselves to accept the doctrine that the prophets and apostles were mistaken about God? Are we going to allow society to tell us that the Bible is outmoded and largely irrelevant and must therefore be reassessed in the light of modern advancements?

Has God changed? Are we going to accept it? Is there a change in the purpose of God? Have the changes in human society startled or shocked God?

Must we, in order to remain intellectually respectable and have good standing with these who doubt the Word, humbly say, "Well, I do not believe in miracles"? Or have we got enough of our Protestant protest and courage to stand up and say, "I believe in miracles whenever God Almighty wants to perform them. I believe that whenever God wants to do anything that is out of the ordinary and contrary to or at least above the common processes of nature, He is able to do it. I believe the miracles of Jesus Christ were real miracles. I believe the miracles of the Old Testament were real miracles." Are we going to allow ourselves to be brainwashed along with all the rest? Or are we going to dare to stand and protest and be known over this country as being Protestants indeed? We would be people who refuse to adjust but who make the world adjust to us.

When you adjust, you are dead. The same is true if a church adjusts to these ideas. If you adjust, you are done. But if you dare to stand, the world will adjust to you. I can promise you that. Not all will adjust to you, but at least some will.

Some have asked themselves, "Is communism the unforeseen and unpredicted invasion? Is that what God did not know about, what Christ did not foresee?" Has Christ, after having come down the centuries triumphant, at last met His Waterloo? What is your answer to that? My answer is a loud, roaring, resounding no! He has never met His Waterloo and He never will. He, the Lord Christ, is going to ride the sky on a white horse, and upon His thigh will be written, "King of kings and Lord of lords." The rich men, the mighty men, the scientists, the doctors and the lords of finance will cry for the rocks and the mountains to fall on them, to hide them from the wrath of the Lamb and the fury of His power.

Have God's people at last been plucked out of His hand? He said we would never be plucked out of His hand, but did He know enough to tell us that? Have there been some new advancements and developments that He did not foresee? The answer again is no!

Shall we surrender?

Shall we surrender to the world? No! Shall we surrender to liberalism? No! Shall we surrender to apostate Protestantism? The answer is no! Shall we surrender to the brainwashed churches whose preachers are afraid to stand up and talk as I am? The answer again is no!

Our church is going to go the way of the gospel. We are not radicals nor fools. We do not fast 40 days. We dress like other people, drive vehicles and have modern homes. We are human and like to laugh. But we believe that God Almighty has not changed and that Jesus Christ is the same. He is victorious, and we do not have to apologize for Him. We do not have to modify, adjust, edit or amend. He stands as the glorious Lord, and nobody needs to apologize for Him.

If our answer to the questions I have asked is yes, then we leave to our children a heritage of nothing but death. I say now, shall we believe the ringing words, "I the LORD do not change" (Malachi 3:6)? I believe them. Shall we believe that "Jesus Christ is the same yesterday and today and forever" (Hebrews 13:8)? I do. We must believe the words that say, "To him who overcomes, I will give the right to eat from the tree of life, which is in the paradise of God" (Revelation 2:7b). "He who overcomes will not be hurt at all by the second death" (2:11b). "To him who overcomes, I will give the right to sit with me on my throne" (3:21a).

We are not going to be sheep running over the precipice because other dumb sheep are running over it. We see the precipice—we know it is there. We are listening to the voice of the shepherd, not the voice of terrified sheep. The terrified, intimidated sheep are going everywhere.

I stand solidly and protest this. I believe we need a reformation back to the belief that God knew what He was talking about in the first place. We need to get back to the belief that Jesus Christ did not miss anything but foresaw it all, back to the belief that the apostles spoke as they were moved by the Holy Spirit. We must return to the belief that our fathers who gave us the great creeds were not fools but wise saints who knew what they were talking about. We must get back to the belief that

Protestants are to protest, dissenters are to dissent and nonconformists must refuse to conform.

How the covenanters stood

Read history and see how the covenanters stood and died rather than give up to the enemy. Are we satisfied to be degenerate sons of great fathers? Consider A.B. Simpson who walked the shores of the Atlantic Ocean with cardboard in the soles of his shoes because he did not have money to buy new ones. He prayed and groaned in spirit and cried to God for people of all nations who had not heard the gospel. He prayed "Oh God, I believe Jesus Christ thy Son is the same yesterday, today and forever." We are his descendants, but we ought to spend a day in sackcloth and ashes.

At 36, Simpson was a Presbyterian preacher so sick that he said, "I feel I could fall into the grave when I have a funeral." He could not preach for months at a time because of his sickness. He went to a little camp meeting in the woods and heard a quartet sing, "No man can work like Jesus/ No man can work like Him." Simpson went off among the pine trees with that ringing in his heart: "Nobody can work like Jesus; nothing is too hard for Jesus. No man can work like Him." The learned, stiffnecked Presbyterian threw himself down upon the pine needles and said, "If Jesus Christ is what they said He was in the song, heal me."

The Lord healed him, and he lived to be 76 years old. Simpson founded a society that is now one of the largest evangelical denominations in the world, The Christian and Missionary Alliance.

We are his descendants and we sing his songs. But are we going to allow ourselves to listen to that which will modify our faith, practices and beliefs, water down our gospel and dilute the power of the Holy Spirit? I, for one, am not!

I am cheered to know so many of you are with me on this. We are going to go to the New Testament and be Bible Christians. We are going to sell out to God and not the devil. We are going to pray more, read our Bibles more and attend prayer meeting more. We are going to give more and break bad habits by the power of God. We are going to become Christians after God's heart. We are going to be protesters in an hour when the smooth, sickly, slippery, rotten, backslidden, degenerate, apostate Christianity is accepted. We are going to stand for God, to act like simple Protestant Christians, to act like our Presbyterian Scottish forebears, to act like our English Methodist forebears, to act like the dear old Baptist who broke the ice in the creek and baptized people in the freezing water. They had a saying in those days, "Nobody ever caught a cold getting baptized in the ice." God Almighty saw to it that nobody ever died of pneumonia.

Those Protestant forebears made these two nations, the United States and Canada. They made this continent. Are we going to be descendants of which they should be ashamed? Or are we going to say, "Lead on, we are following. You followed Jesus Christ, and we are following you."

John Thomas was a dear old Welsh preacher I used to hear. While he preached he would raise his hands and say, "You supply the grit and God will supply the grace." He was right. You've got the grit; God has the grace.

Two Portraits
of the Church

*So he said to me, "This is the word of the LORD
to Zerubbabel: 'Not by might nor by power, but by
my Spirit,' says the LORD Almighty." (Zechariah
4:6)*

On our farm in Pennsylvania there were
cherry trees which were attacked by little
parasites of some sort. A parasite would get
into a little branch, pierce the bark and exude a
gum. Then the branch would get a knot on it
and bend. All over the trees were those little
bent places with gummy knots. After two or
three years, those cherry trees would not
bloom. If they did, the blooms usually dropped
early and the cherries did not come to fruition.
If the blooms did not drop early, the cherries
would be flat and undeveloped or only red on
one side.

My father was not too interested in fruit. He
was interested in cattle, horses and grain. If my
father had known how he could have protected

those trees before they got into that wretched condition and properly sprayed or treated them, he could have gotten rid of the worms and bugs and saved the trees and fruit.

I believe that a pastor who is content with a vineyard that is not at its best is not a good husbandman. It is my prayer that we may be a healthy and fruitful vineyard and that we may be an honor to the Well Beloved, Jesus Christ the Lord, that He might go before the Father and say, "These are mine for whom I pray, and they have heard the Word and have believed on Me." I pray that we might fit into the high priestly prayer of John 17, that we would be a church after Christ's own heart so that in us He might see the travail of His soul and be satisfied.

In order for us to be a vine like that, there must be basic purity. Each one must have a great purity of heart. I believe that there are no emotional experiences that do not rest upon great purity of heart. No one can impress me or interest me in any kind of spiritual manipulation if his or her heart is not pure—even if it is raising the dead. Sound righteousness in conduct must be at the root of all valid spiritual experience.

A new wave of religion

I am afraid of a new wave of religion that has come. It started in the United States, and it is spreading. It is a sort of esoteric affair of the soul or the mind, and there are strange phenomena that attend it. I am afraid of anything that does not require purity of heart on the part of individuals and righteousness of conduct in life.

I also long in the tender mercies of Christ that among us there may be the following:

1. *A beautiful simplicity.* I am wary of the artificialness and complexities of religion. I would like to see simplicity. Our Lord Jesus was one of the simplest men who ever lived. You could not involve Him in anything formal. He said what He had to say as beautifully and as naturally as a bird sings on the bough in the morning. That is what I would like to see restored to the churches. The opposite of that is artificiality and complexity.

2. *A radiant Christian love.* I want to see a restoration of a radiant Christian love so it will be impossible to find anyone who will speak unkindly or uncharitably about another or to another. This is carefully thought out and carefully prayed through. The devil would have a spasm. He would be so chagrined that he would sulk in his self-made hell for years. There should be a group of Christians with radiant love in this last worn-out dying period of the Christian dispensation, a people so loving that you could not get them to speak unkindly and you could not get them to speak uncharitably.

3. *A feeling of humble reverence.* I am disap-

pointed that we come to church without a sense of God or a feeling of humble reverence. There are false religions, strange religious cults and Christian cults that think they have God in a box someplace, and when they approach that box they feel a sense of awe. Of course, you and I want to be saved from all paganism and false cultism. But we would also like to see a company of people who were so sure that God was with them, not in a box or in a biscuit, but in their midst. They would know that Jesus Christ was truly among them to a point that they would have a sense of humble reverence when they gathered together.

4. *An air of joyous informality.* The great English preacher who was pastor for many years of Westminster Chapel in London, G. Campbell Morgan, left his church and went down to Wales where the Welsh revival was going on under Evan Roberts earlier in this century. He stayed there awhile and soaked up the glory of it. I read the sermon that he preached to his congregation afterward, and it was as near to scolding as that great preacher ever got. He said to them, "Your singing is joyless, your demeanor is joyless, and you do not have the lift or joy that I saw in Wales." He urged them that they might get into a place where that sense of joyous informality might be upon them.

5. *A place where each esteems others better than himself or herself.* As a result of that, everyone

should be willing to serve, but nobody would be jockeying for position. Nothing is quite so bitterly humorous as ambition in the church of Christ. It would be as though a man who was on a lifeboat being saved from certain salty death in the ocean depths should become ambitious to become captain of the little boat on its way to save those on board. It is as though a man were to enter a disaster area where an earthquake had hit and people were dying and would fight for a high position there.

No place for the ambitious or lazy

The church of Christ is no place for the ambitious or the lazy. I would like to see our Christian communion be a place where each one esteems the other better than himself or herself. For that reason, nobody should push and nobody should jockey for position. On the other hand, nobody should refuse to serve.

6. *A childlike candor.* I love children because of their unbelievably beautiful candor. They look at you and say the most utterly simple things. If they were just a little older they would blush to the roots of their hair, but they are utterly and completely candid. I like to talk with them and have them come up and chat with me because they are bound to tell me things before they leave. If you do not want it told, do not tell the little ones because they just tell anything. They do not have anything to hide. I believe that with the limitations proper

to our adult years we ought to be at a place where spiritually we should be so candid there would be no duplicity, no dishonesty.

A duplex is a house where there is more than one dwelling; there are two dwellings. Duplicity is the same thing—it means two. Judas Iscariot, for instance, was duplicity incarnated. He was so slick that even the disciples did not know which one was the traitor. They said, "Lord, is it I?" And Jesus said, "There's the man. When he dips into the dish you'll know him." He had to tell them. This son of perdition had lived with Jesus and His 11 disciples for three years and had fooled them so completely that they did not know which one was the traitor when the showdown came. They had to have a little sign to indicate. That was the slickest piece of duplicity I know about. He was two-faced, and he could change faces with the occasion. He was so slick in the change that nobody caught on. He showed one face to Jesus and His disciples and the other to the enemies of Jesus. Now that is duplicity.

A people without duplicity

In Christian communion we ought to be a people without duplicity. Each one of us has only one face. I know that if you have more than one face to present to the public, something is desperately wrong. One of your faces is going to fall under an awful judgment of God.

We must be without duplicity, dishonesty

and hypocrisy. What is hypocrisy? *Hypocrisy* is an old Greek word used for an actor on stage, somebody who pretended to be what he or she was not. He was not Job but he pretended to be Job, so he put on a mask of some sort and strutted around the stage. People do it today, too. They get up on the theater stage or on TV, glue whiskers on and put on makeup to become people they are not. A hypocrite is an actor, somebody who is playing a part.

7. *A presence of Christ that is as the fragrance of myrrh and aloes.* When you become accustomed to the smell of His garments you will be spoiled for anything less. If we never smell the myrrh and aloes out of the ivory palaces, we may go along a lifetime and not miss it. But one beautiful whiff of the fragrance of these garments and we will never be satisfied with anything less.

When my wife and I were first married we attended a church of The Christian and Missionary Alliance in Akron, Ohio. There was something on that church, a sense of the fragrance of God. The great Dr. Gerow preached there in those days. The church had some sweet Christian brethren, some wonderful men and women of God, and there was a fragrance on that place. I have never forgotten it. I was between 19 and 21 for the three years I spent in that church, and I do not remember getting help from others of my age. But how I remember getting help that is with me to this day from the older saints whose garments were fragrant with the myrrh, aloes and cassia out of the ivory palaces!

8. *Answers to prayer; miracles should not be uncommon.* I am not a miracle preacher. I have been in churches where they announced miracle meetings. If you look in the Saturday newspaper you will see occasionally somebody who will hit town and announce, "Come out and see some miracles." That kind of performing I do not care for.

You cannot get miracles as you would get a chemical reaction. You cannot get a miracle as you get a wonderful act on stage by a magician. God does not sell Himself into the hands of religious magicians. I do not believe in that kind of miracles. I believe in the kind of miracles that God gives to His people who live so close to Him that answers to prayer are common and these miracles are not uncommon.

John Wesley never lowered himself to preach miracles once in his life. But the miracles that followed John Wesley's ministry were unbelievable. On one instance he had to make an engagement, and his horse fell lame and could not travel. Wesley got down on his knees beside his horse and prayed for its healing. Then he got back up and rode, without the horse limping, to where he was going. He did not publicize the miracle and say, "We'll have a big tent here and advertise it." God just did those things for him.

While C.H. Spurgeon did not preach healing, he had more people delivered in answer to his prayer than any doctor in London. Those are the kinds of miracles I am talking about.

In light of the Scripture, in light of the Judgment Seat of Christ and in light of eternity, is what I am asking unreasonable? Is the description I have given unreasonable? Is this portrait of a true church an unreasonable portrait? Is it undesirable and impossible that we should have this kind of church? Is this an unscriptural picture?

The church should be a healthy, fruitful vineyard that will bring honor to Christ, a church after Christ's own heart where He can look at the travail of His soul and be satisfied. Among the people should be a beautiful simplicity and a radiant Christian love so it would be impossible to find gossips and talebearers. There should be a feeling of humble reverence and an air of joyous informality, where each one esteems others better than himself or herself, where everyone is willing to serve but no one jockeys to serve. Childlike candor without duplicity or dishonesty should mark the church, and the presence of Christ should be felt and the fragrance of His garments smelled by His beloved. Prayers should be answered so regularly that we think nothing of it. It would be common because God is God, and we are

His people. When necessary, miracles would not be uncommon.

Is that, in the light of Scripture, unreasonable and undesirable to expect of a church? Is there something better? If there is something better, you name it!

Is this impossible? Is anything impossible with God? Is anything impossible where the Lord Jesus Christ is? Is this unscriptural? No! The only thing that is unscriptural about this vision is that it is not up to the standard of Scripture yet. The scriptural standards are still high.

If you answer, "No, it is not unreasonable, undesirable or impossible," then you are saying you believe in this. If you believe in this, if you would like to become the church that could begin this reformation, this change toward the better, this recapturing of the ancient power of God in the souls of people, then there must be a radical psychological break with the prevailing religious mood.

I have told you by careful description what a church ought to be. Now I am going to describe churches as they are, with beautiful exceptions, of course. There are pure saints in almost all the churches, a few here and there, but the prevailing religious mood is self-centered instead of world-centered. Instead of being outgoing and soul-winning, the average church is self-centered and self-satisfied. We make our reports and we spend pages telling what wonderful good boys and nice girls we have been. Self-satisfaction seems to be upon us all.

Worldliness of spirit is the prevailing mood in the average church, along with carnality of heart. To the Corinthians, Paul said in effect, "You are carnal and I cannot speak to you of spiritual matters. I would like to come to preach deep things to you, but you are too carnal."

Another prevailing mood of the average church is to be Christian in name but in practice to be unchristian. Our trouble is not that we refuse to believe right doctrine, but we refuse to practice it. We have the peculiar contradiction of believing the right thing and living the wrong way, a strange anomaly within the church everywhere.

In the church many are lovers of pleasure more than lovers of God. If you do not like what I am saying, I want to ask you something. Think about the company you run with. What do they talk about most? God and the love of God, or other things? You decide that.

Many Christians today will not endure sound doctrine. Paul described these people as having "itching ears" (2 Timothy 4:3). They did not like sound doctrine, but they were Christians. They called themselves Christians, but their ears were itchy.

A commentator I read some years back explained this. In Paul's day the pigs had a disease called "itching ears." The symptom was that their ears got inflamed and itched terribly. The only way they could get relief from these inflamed ears was to go to a pile of rocks and rub their ears earnestly and vigorously. The stones scratched their ears for the time being.

Paul saw that, smiled a sad smile and said, "I am running into Christians here and there who are just like that. They love pleasure more than God and will not endure sound doctrine. They have itching ears so they will be eager for something else beside the sound doctrine and holy ways. They will pile up teachers everywhere and rub their ears for dear life." That is a most dramatic and colorful illustration. A lot of so-called Christians have to have piles of rocks to rub their ears. They will not endure sound doctrine. I think that is a description of the churches, Protestant and evangelical.

In the light of New Testament predictions, teachings and standards, is what I just said about the prevailing religious mood untrue? Is what I have said about the prevailing religious mood uncharitable? Is it extreme? I do not think it is, but I only ask you to do one thing: Look around you and look in your own heart. See which of these pictures describes the churches you know.

A Biblical Concept
of the Church

Around the beginning of World War I we
had a visitation in the United States, not
of spiritual power, but of what I have named
tabernacleism. Anyone with a good personality
and preaching ability would start a tabernacle
around the corner, get a crowd, pull out of the
churches and proceed to poke fun at the churches. I can understand why there was such a
revolt—the churches were pretty dead. A lot of
money was spent to build these tabernacles,
but often the men who founded them left town
and nobody else could keep them up, so the
crowds wandered away. The mortgage holders
foreclosed, and the tabernacles were left high
and dry.

The depression killed the movement. Nobody
had any money, so it did not pay to go around
starting churches. As a result, however, today
we have immense church buildings throughout
the United States. They are not good for anything, but they left behind a residue—a bad

and dangerous philosophy. This philosophy is actually a dangerous theology regarding the church. The church was thrown out and said to be of no account—come when you please, go when you must; hold no creed but Christ, no law but love, no pastor but Jesus, no membership, no anything. This philosophy has left us high and dry like a shore after a storm when the wind has blown.

It is time for us to reconsider this matter of the church. Most people think of the church as a familiar social fact. Their attitude toward Protestantism generally is that of a matter of course, and people, even average Christians, think they are in favor of the church. They favor the church much the same as they support motherhood, decency and sanitation. It is as accepted as a convention that we never question or doubt. If anybody does question or doubt, they are considered communists or atheists. People will even pour out their money to support social convention.

But I wonder how many ever sit down and say, "What is this? Maybe the church is just something that is here; it doesn't have any value and doesn't have any reason for being here." How many present-day Christians have ever searched the Scripture with a serious burden on their hearts to know what the church is? Is it simply a convention that is carried on? How many Christians have ever prayed earnestly for light from heaven about it?

It seems that the average person spends more time and intellectual labor each year filling out income tax forms than he or she spends in a lifetime trying to learn from the Scriptures and from the light of the Spirit what the church is and what he or she ought to do about it. Why is it in the world? What did Jesus mean when He said, "On this rock I will build my church, and the gates of Hades will not overcome it" (Matthew 16:18b)? If people were to chew their pencils and walk the floor and go out for a walk and come back and work on it and search and think and discern and divide and go through all that they have to go through to make out their income taxes every year, I believe that they could come up with some wonderful answers.

Must understand the universal church

When we know what the universal church is, we will understand what a local church is. The average local church is to a large extent a social organization where well-intentioned people get together and know each other. They are drawn together by coffee, tea, friendship, skating parties and things like that. Those things are harmless. But when we know what the church really is, we will understand that while these things are all right on the margin of the church, they are not the purpose of it.

Meeting, shaking hands and drinking coffee are perfectly legitimate if we do not need them—they are not what holds us together. But when those activities are what hold us together, we do not have a church; we have something else. Unfortunately, we might as well admit it: That is often all that the churches have.

First we have to have a philosophy about the church. What is the church? I want to use three illustrations to show what the true Church of Jesus Christ is.

The bride of Christ

First, the church is the bride of Christ. Jesus was a complete man. He had all the nature of a man, but He never married. He could have, but He never did. He never married any woman though He was a true and complete man. He never married a daughter of a woman that He might marry His whole church, the bride.

A true local church is the bride of Christ in recapitulation, in miniature. Everything that is in the whole church of Christ should be recapitulated in the local church. The church, part of it in heaven and part of it on earth, is the bride of Christ. Our Lord Jesus washed His bride, regenerated her and prepared her. He is coming back to take her—the whole church—as His bride.

But any local church is the whole church in recapitulation, just as a local election recapitulates a national one. The same liberty is expressed. The same candidates run. They talk about each other; they plead their own worth and put up bulletins and do the same thing on a small scale that they do on the federal level. That may be a poor illustration, but the whole bride of Christ is recapitulated. Any local church is what the whole church is, just in miniature.

> Husbands, love your wives, just as Christ loved the church and gave himself up for her to make her holy, cleansing her by the washing with water through the word, and to present her to himself as a radiant church, without stain or wrinkle or any other blemish, but holy and blameless. In this same way, husbands ought to love their wives as their own bodies. He who loves his wife loves himself. After all, no one ever hated his own body, but he feeds and cares for it, just as Christ does the church. (Ephesians 5:25–29)

This figure drawn from husbands and wives is applied directly without apology to Jesus Christ and His church. Just as a young man would not marry a dirty bride, so Jesus Christ will not marry a church that has stains or wrinkles or blemishes. His desire is for a glorious church, and He wants to love that church as a man loves his own bride.

There was a man named Adam, and he was the first bachelor. God told Adam to call in all the animals and name them. According to the Bible, names were given after the nature of the animals. Adam named the bear after the bear nature and the lion after the lion nature. Then the Bible makes this touching comment—"But for Adam no suitable helper was found" (Genesis 2:20b). Some people think that just means there was no woman yet. But what it means is that God and Adam had not found any nature like Adam's yet. Adam had to have someone who was satisfactory for him. No one was worthy of him. There had to be somebody with his nature. There was no one appropriate because the rest were the beasts of the field and the fowls of the air—they did not have the same nature as Adam, who was made in the image of God.

God told Adam to lie down. Adam obeyed and went into a deep sleep. There in a state of deep anesthesia, God operated on the man and took from his chest a rib. God then fashioned the rib into a woman, gave her life and called her woman—the life-giver, who shall give life to all the race. When Adam came out of his sleep, he looked around and saw Eve. She looked good in his sight. Adam knew Eve, she conceived a son and thus the race began.

But then there was another Adam. First Corinthians 15 tells us about a second Adam, the last Adam, Jesus Christ the Lord. He had a nature that was divine. He was divine, God in flesh. Jesus was a perfect and complete man, but He married no daughter of woman. He married no daughter of woman because there was none found worthy of Him.

Just as He had done with Adam, God put Jesus on the cross in a deep sleep and opened His side. Out from His side flowed not a rib but water and blood. From that water and blood God is washing, cleansing and preparing a bride worthy of Jesus. God did not create Eve from nothing as He had Adam, but He created her from the wounded side of Adam. Even so, the Lord is not creating a race that does not now exist to be His church. He takes the race that now exists—certain members of it—and washes it in the blood that came from the wounded side. By the Holy Spirit, He gives the nature of Christ to the bride, so she will be worthy of Him.

There was not among the daughters of Eve one that was appropriate and satisfactory for Jesus. Therefore He is preparing Himself a bride who has His nature, as Eve had the nature of the husband out of whose side she came. A theologian once noted that God took the bone that made the woman not from Adam's head, that she might lord it over him; not from his feet, that he might lord it over her; but from his heart, that she might understand him, and he might love her. That is what the church is—the bride of Christ.

If you are a member of the true church of Christ, then you are a member of the company that will make up the true bride of Christ. As a local church, we are a miniature of the bride of Christ.

The body of Christ

A second description of the church is the body of Christ. Jesus Christ is the head, and as the head of His church He directs it. My hands move because my head tells them to. My head directs my body. The head of a local church is not the pastor, but Jesus Christ the Lord. He is the head of the universal church of which the local church is a part. A local church is not all the body of Christ, but in miniature it is the body of Christ.

Third, the church is depicted as an ark on the flood waters. As the ark of Noah floated on the waters and contained all who would be salvaged, so the church of Jesus Christ is an ark on the flood waters and contains all who will be salvaged. Remember that! All in the ark are saved, and all outside the ark perish. All around us is a perishing world, and we float on top of it in a little ark called the church. All that are not in the church—the ark—will perish.

You say, "Now hold on a minute. Do you mean to say that if you don't join the Avenue Road Church, you will be lost?" No, but what I do say is that the church is the ark containing the ransomed, and inside the ark is life. Outside the living church of Christ are the lost. Inside are the saved. You are not saved by joining a church, which is a mistake local churches make.

The animals all came into Noah's ark by the door. Christ is the door to the church, and whoever will be saved must come in by the door. There is no other ark on the flood. Suppose someone said, "Well, hold on a minute. Don't be so narrow-minded. Let's be tolerant. We do not want to get in Noah's ark; we want an ark of our own." Well, there weren't any other arks on the flood. It was either get into Noah's ark or perish. A few got into Noah's ark, and God preserved the race.

In the church of Christ, God is salvaging a small number from the flood. A fatal error is the independent life—to say that you are a Christian, but you don't associate with any churches. You are a Christian, but you don't feel the necessity to join a church. It is true that there are hypocrites in the church—not in the true church, but in the local assembly. Even Jesus had His Judas. The local assembly and the true church of Christ are sometimes not synonymous.

Sometimes people come into the local church who have never come into the universal church. People join a church who have never been born into the true church. Some churches actually throw the doors open and say, "Now we'll sing the closing hymn for those who want to unite with the church. Come to the front." Al Capone could come in and join. Nobody asks any questions; they just take in anybody. I do not believe in that at all, and I know you do not either.

Get into the universal church first

I believe that if you are going to get into a local church, you should first be in the universal church, which Jesus purchased with His own blood. You should get into the church with rebirth, the Holy Spirit and regeneration. Then you should join a local assembly. It is impossible to receive Christ and reject His people. How do you find the Shepherd? Go where the sheep are! If you do not know where the Shepherd is, then go where the sheep are. All else being equal, that is where you will find the Shepherd. Whoever receives Christ must receive His people too. Jesus said, "He who receives you receives me" (Matthew 10:40a). Whoever rejects the bride rejects the Bridegroom, and whoever rejects the flock rejects the Shepherd. I think that is clear enough.

Consider this illustration: Two young couples marry in June. One is a Christian couple and takes a serious view of life. Their home is full of love, and they are looking forward to a family. The other two love each other too, in a Hollywood sort of way, and look forward to skin diving, water skiing and just having fun. They do not want any children. In the course of time, after two or three years, both of the women have a little baby; one was wanted and one was not.

Christian parents look at their little baby, their hearts glow and they say, "Isn't she absolutely wonderful?" This first couple feels a sense of sacredness, and so they pray, plan and say, "Wasn't God good to give us this little one?" And she becomes a spiritual gift to them. They know that when she grows up she will be like other people with tantrums, but they take her as a gift from God. Bringing up this little baby becomes a sort of sacrament to them.

The other couple have their baby, and of course they love her, but they never quite see it like the other couple. It never occurs to them to pray, and as soon as she is old enough, they send for a baby-sitter and go on their way. The point is that the first couple understood the sacredness of their baby. The other couple was not thinking of the sacredness of their baby, but rather they were thinking of having fun. They took the baby as a necessary evil that they learned to like after a while.

This illustration also gives you two views of the church. Suppose I do not know what a church is, but I want to come to a church for the social fact and I join it because I think it would be better to join than not. In that case I take the same attitude toward the church as the second couple had toward their baby. The experience does not have the glow of sacredness. But if I see there is a great church being salvaged from the wreckage, just as Noah and his family were salvaged, and the church is found throughout the whole world in local groups, I begin to see the sacredness of the local church.

What a different attitude you will take toward the church! You will say, "How lovely that I ever got in." The church will glow to you and have a sense of sacredness on it. If you find any blemish in the church, you will do what the young Christian couple did with their baby—correct it.

If you want fellowship with the church, if you have not formally joined, there are two ways to do so. One is to pray in public, give money, show enthusiasm and fill out a card. The other is to do first things first—join the universal church—and then also fill out a card.

Public confession

An important part of joining the church is public confession. Why does the Lord want us to make a public confession?

The Bible says,

> "The word is near you; it is in your mouth and in your heart," that is, the word of faith we are proclaiming: That if you confess with your mouth, "Jesus is Lord," and believe in your heart that God raised him from the dead, you will be saved. For it is with your heart that you believe and are justified, and it is with your mouth that

you confess and are saved. (Romans 10:8b–10)

The heart believes and the mouth confesses. Both are necessary to salvation. Even the thief on the cross made his poor pitiful confession.

That is why God wants us to fellowship with each other, get together and tell the world and tell each other—because with the mouth confession is made for salvation. My plea is for those who have never undergone the marvel of the regeneration of new birth to take this seriously. Remember you get into the ark through the door, and Jesus Christ is the door. If you reject the ark, you reject the door, and if you reject the door you perish in the flood.

Must be born into the family

To become a member of the body of Christ and join with the bride of Christ, you must be born into the family of Christ. It happens by believing in your heart that Jesus is Lord and confessing your faith with your mouth to the people. This is reasonable, and I do not understand why anybody should find fault with it.

Suppose you were somewhere in the world, and someone asked you your nationality. Is there anybody here that would be ashamed to say where you were from? Why then should you go through life being secret Christians, too frightened, too scared to say, "I am a Christian"? If Jesus Christ has honored you by finding you and laying His hand on you, you ought never be ashamed of Him. You should be able to stand anywhere at any time and say, "I do not care who knows it. I am a Christian." Be proud.

I want the world to know that I am a Christian. From reading the lives of the saints I know I have a long way to go, and I want you to know that, too! I have a sharp tongue and an abrupt manner, and sometimes I say things that hurt feelings. I do not want to hurt your feelings. Just forgive a fellow who is too dumb to know better. I may not be a good Christian, but I am still a Christian. I am a member of the body of Christ. I am in the ark along with the blessed few who have been honored by God with grace, and for that reason I am not ashamed and I do not want you to be.

We want a separated-from-the-world, heads-up, knees-bent, living church! Sure we can have our skating parties, gatherings and coffees. Nothing is wrong with that, provided we know that we do not need it. These activities are something on the side so we can relax. Jesus Christ is our center, and so the way to get in is by faith and confession.

CHAPTER
13

A Model Church

Church people imitate models, and Christians have had a habit of going off on tangents, following moods, modes and habits. We wish it were different, but down the years we have been like a flock of sheep, everybody following everybody else. We have models and we follow them. The church tends to decline in moral power if it chooses the wrong model or an inadequate model. Now don't interrupt me by saying, "Jesus is our model." I know that He is our model—He ought to be our model. But the simple fact is that He is not. He ought to be the model for the churches, but Jesus Christ has about as much authority in the average Protestant church as I have in the average Catholic church.

I heard about a scientist, Jean Henri Fabre, studying one of the species of caterpillars. He got a huge round vessel, a large crock, and put a lot of caterpillars called army worms around the outside bumper-to-bumper. Then he started them moving. Actually he didn't have to start them—they are called army worms because they are always marching. As far as Fabre could tell, no caterpillar knew where it was going: It was following the tail of the one ahead of it, and the one that was after it followed its tail. Each followed the one ahead until they got clear around to the original one that was following the tail of the one ahead of it. Around and around the crock they went. In nature, army worms march across and through the woods and forest and bushes in a straight line. But because they had been tricked and put on a circular path, they went around and around until one after another they fell off.

In the United States I can take you to beautiful little churches with the doors nailed up—all of those blessed religious army worms that once went around in a circle fell off and were buried in the backyard. Now there is nobody there; they have all fallen off. They ran around, chased each other and took each other for models. Now it is all over and there is nothing left but gravestones, green briers, bats and memories.

The Thessalonican church had taken the right models. Their models were God and Paul the apostle. Because they had taken the right models, other people took them for a model. Paul was proud and happy that other people—including the Macedonians and Achaians—were talking about the Christians at Thessalonica. He said, "Your faith in God has become known everywhere. Therefore we do not need to say anything about it, for they themselves report what kind of reception you gave us. They tell how you turned to God from idols to serve the living and true God" (1 Thessalonians 1:8b–9).

The church at Thessalonica was a model church, and I want it to be the pattern for our church. We are to be a model church, a church that people, when they hear about it, will say is a Christian church if ever one was.

If people will follow other people, then they ought to follow the right kind of people in the right direction. If religious people will parade, then we ought to get them parading in the right way. To a large extent evangelicals have been given wrong models. While we talk about the Lord Jesus and fight for the creeds that say He is the Lord of Glory, He has very little to say among us. Who even pretends to obey the Sermon on the Mount? Some dispensationalists have even ruled it out, so it is not even theologically necessary to believe it anymore. It belongs to some other dispensation. That kind of rules out the whole business. Who even pretends to obey the First Corinthians epistle dealing with marriage, litigation and the Lord's Supper?

Features of a model church

The model church must embody certain features. An important one is following the order of the New Testament by letting Scripture decide matters.

I knew a man from India who got hold of a New Testament, was converted and started to preach, but he had no background at all. That is, he started from scratch. He did not have a Greek Orthodox or Roman Catholic or Protestant background. He just started from the beginning. He didn't know anything about churches. He testified, "What I did when I had a problem in the church was to go straight to the New Testament and settle it. I let the New Testament tell me what I was to do." The result was that God greatly blessed him and his work in the land of India.

This is what I would like to see in our church—the New Testament order of letting Scripture decide matters. When it comes to a question—any question—what does the Word of God say? All beliefs and practices should be tested by the Word; no copying unscriptural church methods. We should let the Word of God decide.

I would also have in our body the power of the Spirit of Christ. I have said that the average gospel church could get along without the Holy Spirit—and many do. We are praying for revival. What is revival? It is when the Holy Spirit takes over the work that is His, instead of being pushed aside into the benediction. He now becomes the Chief Executive of the church, running it. "But you will receive power when the Holy Spirit comes on you" (Acts 1:8a). That means that the Spirit of heaven should come to a company on earth with His all-prevailing gifts, power and grace, with His life, His illumination and His discernment. This is not fanaticism; this is not any weird religion. This is just what the Bible teaches.

As a church we must also embody in a supreme degree the purposes for which we exist. There are three purposes for which we exist on earth: to worship, to witness and to work. When people are converted they immediately change their citizenships. They are no longer citizens of earth except in a provisory way. They are now citizens of heaven.

Abraham, when he went down from Ur of the Chaldees, was called a Hebrew, a man from the other side of the river, a stranger. He spoke with an accent. He brought different habits: eating habits, dressing habits, speech habits and other customs. He brought them from Ur of the Chaldees. He was a different man, a stranger and a foreigner there.

We immediately switch citizenship

Christians, when they are born of God, immediately shift their citizenships and become pilgrims and strangers where they used to be citizens. "I am a stranger here/ upon a foreign land/ my home is far away/ beyond the golden strand," we used to sing. Why then does God leave us here? Why are we here at all? All who are born anew have new natures. God becomes our Father and Jesus becomes our Brother, we become the habitation of the Spirit and heaven is our fatherland. Why then are we left here on earth among strangers? We are left here to worship, to witness and to work. Those three things are what we are here for.

We are here to worship

Our worship must be in the Spirit. Jesus said, "God is spirit, and his worshipers must worship in spirit and in truth" (John 4:24). To worship in such a way that God will accept it, there must be individual committal to Christ and inward purification by blood and fire. There must be separation from the world, from its opinions, habits and values. But right now we are just coming out of a period when people were so eager to make converts that they fell into a trap that Jesus Christ warned them about. He said, "You travel over land and sea to win a single convert, and when he becomes one, you make him twice as much a son of hell as you are" (Matthew 23:15b).

We are just coming through that period when John 3:16 was the only verse anybody used. The Lord loves everybody. Come, come, come; everybody get converted. So people came, but their conversions were backward. In place of the people being converted into the kingdom of God, the church was converted over to their habits and ways. There was no separation from the world; the world's opinions and habits came into the church.

Do you want God to bless you? You say, "We want God to bless us. We believe the Lord is coming." Did you read the Bible or watch TV more this week? Think of the time you have spent. How many half-hour periods did you spend with your Bible, and how many did you spend with amusements? We do not take our faith seriously enough.

We are here to witness

We are here to worship; we are here to get rid of the habits and values of the world; and we are here to witness. What is a witness? A witness is somebody who testifies to a personal experience. Have you ever thought of the unscriptural, hopeless situation we are in now in evangelical churches? The preacher is the only soul-winner. If he does not come through and win souls, the church declines. The Lord never meant it to be so. He meant that everybody should be a witness.

What should we be witnesses to? We are witnesses only to our personal experiences. Go into a court of law and say, "Well, Aunt Mabel told me ... " and they will shut you up immediately. We do not care what Aunt Mabel said. What do *you* know? What did you see? What did you feel? What did you hear? What did you taste? What came within the confines of your personal experience? The Lord says, "You will be my witnesses" (Acts 1:8b). Go tell everybody.

But suppose somebody says, "How do you know?" Then we can smile and say, "I was there—I know." I was converted, and I know I was converted. I was present, so I know. Nobody can argue me out of it.

When I was young, I used to read books dealing with atheism. I tried to acquaint myself as best I could with everything that was against Christianity. I deliberately bought and read books aimed to prove that Christianity was not true, that the Bible was a hoax, that Jesus Christ was a myth and that the whole thing was subjective self-deception. When I had read the books I could not answer them. I did not know how to answer them, but I knew one thing. "Hold on a minute," I would say to the authors. "I happen to know. I was there. You are trying to argue me down by reasoning, but I can tell you by experience that I know." More than one time, I got on my knees and with tears near the surface worshiped Jesus Christ, God's Son. I did not know the answers to their arguments, but I knew the One against whom they were arguing. A witness is somebody who has been there and who knows by experience.

We are here to work

The third reason we are in the world is to do good works. They call that benevolence in the churches. A fellow drives up in an expensive car, his wife gets out wearing a genuine fur coat, he parks and finally wanders in wearing a fine wool suit. The church members pass around a plate for benevolence and he puts in a dime. We owe the world good works. God anointed Jesus Christ with the Holy Spirit and power, and Jesus went about doing good and healing all who were oppressed by the devil. Jesus did good works and said, "As the Father has sent me, I am sending you" (John 20:21b). You and I are in the world not to put a thin, apologetic dime in the basket, but we are here to share with others around the world.

I pray to God Almighty that I may not live my life out and when I am gone not have anybody sorry I went. It is entirely possible. Doing good works is not just benevolence, either. It is doing good works for Jesus Christ's sake. That is why you are left here. Otherwise you would be in heaven, sitting around tuning your harp. Instead you are down here doing good works.

How do I do good works? I do them by prayer and by my money. There is a beautiful passage where Jesus tells a parable and then explains it. He says, "Use worldly wealth to gain friends for yourselves, so that when it is gone, you will be welcomed into eternal dwellings" (Luke 16:9b). The stingiest old miser that ever lived only needs two pennies when he is dead—one for each eye. In other words, by the right and generous use of my money I can bless people whom I have never seen. When the end comes and money does not help me anymore, there will be people there and God will say to them, "This is the man who kept you two years when you were a displaced child over there. His money helped you." They never knew who it was. Good works are beautiful, and churches ought to be doing them.

Is it fanaticism that a church ought to worship, to witness and to work? I do not think so. If we do those three things rightly we will have very little time left for anything else.

Suppose someone asks, "What do you do?" There are all sorts of things you can do. You can pray and you can watch for God's providential openings. You can do good works and follow Jesus who was anointed with the Holy Spirit to do good works.

Must be a change in way of life

Here is what grieves me, and I believe this also grieves the Holy Spirit: My hearers rise to this call emotionally, but they will not confirm it by a corresponding change in their way of life. Their goodness is like the morning clouds—by 9:00 o'clock the sun has burnt off the fog. This is what happens to many people's good intentions. They rise emotionally to an urgent message that we become a New Testament church, that we become a model church, that we have the order of the New Testament and the power of the Holy Spirit in order that we might worship, work and witness. Emotionally they rise to it, but they will not confirm their emotions by corresponding changes in their way of life.

They want to be blessed by God, but they want God to bless them on their terms. They look pensively to God for victory, but they will not bring their giving into line. They will not practice family prayer, rushing off without it. They will not take time for secret prayer and will not forgive those who have wronged them. They will not seek to be reconciled to those with whom they have quarreled. They will not pick up their crosses and say, "Jesus, I my cross have taken, all to leave and follow Thee."

What is going to bring about the model church? Do you think that it ever can come within a church? Is there too much dead wood? Are there too many wrong directions, or too many things wrong with us? Are we like an old person who has every organ in the body gone bad? The doctor looks the person over and says, "There is nothing I can do for you. Go home and wait." Are we like that? Or is there hope?

I believe there is hope. It is going to cost a little bit. In fact, it is going to cost quite a bit. "If anyone would come after me, he must deny himself and take up his cross and follow me" (Matthew 16:24b). It is never fun carrying a cross. Isn't it strange that Jesus made a bloody, pain-filled cross a symbol of His religion?

Modern churches have made fun a symbol of their religion. I want to grieve, bury my head in my hands and sob before God when I hear, as I often do, precious young people whom I would give my blood for, get up and in a little tiny voice say, "Oh, I am so glad I have found out that you do not have to be a sinner to have fun. We have fun in the church, too. You can follow Jesus and have fun." Then they sit down. How they have been betrayed! It is the cross that is the symbol of the Christian life. But we will not pick up our cross. We will not forgive our enemies. We will not be reconciled.

A raking of carnal dead leaves

The average church is simply a raking together of carnal, dead leaves, without any life. We organize it, give to support it and keep it up. Still we have nothing but carnal leaves that will burn in hell in the days before us when our Lord returns.

I believe there is hope, and I believe there is a lot of it. It is going to take a bit of grit and determination and a good deal of prayer and cross-bearing. But we will have God on our side, and I would rather have God on my side than all the armies of the world. He will confirm the word of His servant; He will perform the counsel of His messenger. "I will turn the darkness into light before them and make the rough places smooth. These are the things I will do; I will not forsake them" (Isaiah 42:16b).

He will give fruit if we will but trust Him and dare to believe. Have you got the Christian courage to change your home to suit the will of God? Have you got the Christian courage to bring your business into line with the will of God? Have you got the Christian courage to bring your personal life into line with the will of God, to purge everything that is not of God? We have yet to know how desperately we need God to do something in this terrible day in which we live, a day of worldliness, carnality, competition and vainglory. How we need God; how we need Christ; how we need the Holy Spirit. We need clean living, sanctification and purity of heart. Then the Spirit of the Living God will come upon us.

Some say, "This is a gloomy business you are preaching." When the Moravians went through this, they were anointed of God. Historians said of them that they went out from the church not knowing whether they were still on earth or had already died and gone to heaven. The joy of the Lord was radiantly beautiful upon them, and they became happy people.

"John Wesley," Dr. Johnson said, "was the greatest example of sheer moral happiness that I ever knew." I am not preaching a gloomy religion to you. I am only telling you there must be a new direction set. We must seek the Lord. One glimpse of His face will take away all our carnal desires for anything less than that.

Then the hungry-hearted, the thirsty, the disillusioned, the disappointed and the sick will come our way. They will come because they will want to come, and they will know why they are coming. They will not come because a person invited them but because of Christ Jesus. The church will begin to grow. It will grow in power, in grace, in numbers, in usefulness, in prestige and in influence. Everybody will know it is the church that the Lord has blessed.

As written in Isaiah 60, God said about Jerusalem, in effect, "I am going to bless you. I am going to put a crown on you and I am going to send my blessings over you like doves to their nest. Everybody that passes by will point and say 'That is the city which the Lord has blessed.'" That is what I want to see in our church. We should become the kind of church that the Lord has blessed. This is the reformation necessary within Protestantism.

God has His seed of survival. He has His people who are ready to say, "God, we want to have biblical order, and we want to have the power of the Holy Spirit. We want to fulfill Your will in worship, witness and work. We are willing to back up our desires by carrying the cross and by bringing our lives into line with Your desires."

CHAPTER
14

The Voice of Faith

But now, this is what the LORD says—
  he who created you, O Jacob,
  he who formed you, O Israel:
"Fear not, for I have redeemed you;
  I have summoned you by name; you are mine.
When you pass through the waters,
  I will be with you;
and when you pass through the rivers,
  they will not sweep over you.
When you walk through the fire,
  you will not be burned;
  the flames will not set you ablaze.
For I am the LORD, your God,
  the Holy One of Israel, your Savior.
  (Isaiah 43:1–3)

What God has ever done for anyone He will do for anybody else. Let us get a hold of this and not write the lives of our fathers and gild the sepulchers of the ones who have gone before, imagining that we live in a vacuum, void of those who have experienced God. Anything God ever did for anyone in faith He will do for anyone else who meets His conditions.

The voice of unbelief says, "Yes, I'm a believer. I believe the Bible. I don't like those modernists, liberals and modern scientists who deny the Bible. I would not do that for the world. I believe in God, and I believe that God will bless." That is, He will bless at some other time, in some other place and some other people. Those are three sleepers that bring the work of God to a halt. We are believers and we can quote the creed with approval. We believe it, but we believe that God will bless some other people, some other place, some other time—but not now, not here and not us.

Here is the problem: We have to have faith if God is going to do anything for us. Faith is the vitamin that makes all we take from the Bible digestible and makes us able to receive it and assimilate it. If we do not have faith, we cannot get anything. If we allow the gloomy voice of unbelief to whisper to us that God will bless some other time but not now, some other place but not here, some other people but not us, we might as well turn off the lights because nobody will get anywhere.

The voice of faith, however, has quite another message for us. The voice of faith speaks up brightly, though reverently, and says, "Anything God promised and did at any time in any place for anybody God will do for us here if we will meet His conditions." This is basic. When

God speaks, His message has more than one application. If it is truth, it is true for anybody who would believe it anywhere, anytime. Two times two equals four whether it is 400 B.C. or A.D. 1963, whether in Russia, in China or in Canada. Two times two equals four. No one can get around it; anybody can trust it. Nobody can dispensationalize it away. It is an unchanging principle.

When God speaks and His mighty voice thunders down the years, He speaks to His people called Israel and He speaks to His people called Christians. Nothing has happened to invalidate His promises. We must remember that. Nothing in history would invalidate the promises of God. Nothing in philosophy, nothing that science has ever discovered can invalidate His promises. Certainly there have been social changes, and people look at things differently now than they did in other times. Nevertheless, nothing changes God, His promises, human nature, God's purposes or His intentions toward His people, so we can take the Word of God and say, "Here is a living Word."

The first sentence of the Scripture passage says, "This is what the LORD says." Many Bible translations print the word *Lord* in capital letters. This indicates that the Hebrew word used is Jehovah or Yahweh.

The name *Yahweh* is sometimes called the Tetragrammaton. It is so sacred that ancient

Jews would not even speak it. It was the name God spoke out of the fire to Moses when He said, "I am who I am" (Exodus 3:14). That is who is speaking in this passage. Can He make good on His intentions? He certainly can.

Seven names with Jehovah

In our hymnody, books of devotion and important books of theology there are seven names that God gives in compound with Jehovah.

First, *Jehovah-jireh* means "the LORD will provide." If the people of God would remember this, "I am who I am" will provide. He who laid the foundation of the earth, who stretched the heavens above like a curtain and who looks upon the nations and sees them as dust in the balance will provide.

Second, *Jehovah-rapha* means "the LORD who heals you." This is the expression that A.B. Simpson picked up and gave meaning to so it could shine through again. "I am the Lord who heals you." We do not see much or hear much about that now. The doctrine of divine healing is divided into two classes: those who are making a circus out of it, and the discouraged people who are trying to believe and take pills to beat sickness. There is very little of real knowledge of *Jehovah-rapha*, the God who heals, anymore.

Then there is *Jehovah-nissi*, "the LORD our banner"; *Jehovah-shalom*, "The LORD our peace";

Jehovah-ro'i, "the LORD our shepherd"; *Jehovah-tsidkenu*, "the LORD our righteousness"; and *Jehovah-shammah*, "the LORD is present here." This is the mighty God who is speaking, and He wants to get through to you.

Fed trash too many times

Do you know you have been fed trash instead of truth too many times? Do you know you have been betrayed and sold downriver instead of being fed the Living Word of God in too many instances? God is trying to get through to you in His Word, and He says, "I am Jehovah. You are looking to me now. Look away from other people; look to me."

Who are the people we look to? They may be young and good-looking today, but tomorrow they will be old and crack-voiced. But the great God Almighty does not die. "I am Jehovah; I am your righteousness; I am your shepherd; I am your peace; I am your banner of victory; I am your healer; I am your provider; I am present in your midst." This is the One with whom you are dealing. If you would only dare to rise, shake your head and say, "I dare to believe this," you would find the truths of God begin to glow like the stars. You would have life where you have not life, light where you have not light and joy where you have not joy.

What did God do?

"I, even I, am the LORD,

and apart from me there is no savior.
I have revealed and saved and
      proclaimed—
  I, and not some foreign god among you.
You are my witnesses," declares the
      LORD, "that I am God.
  Yes, and from ancient days I am he.
No one can deliver out of my hand.
  When I act, who can reverse it?"

This is what the LORD says—
  your Redeemer, the Holy One of Israel:
"For your sake I will send to Babylon
  and bring down as fugitives all the
      Babylonians,
  in the ships in which they took pride.
I am the LORD, your Holy One,
  Israel's Creator, your King."

This is what the LORD says—
  he who made a way through the sea,
  a path through the mighty waters,
who drew out the chariots and horses,
  the army and reinforcements together,
and they lay there, never to rise again,
  extinguished, snuffed out like a wick.
    (Isaiah 43:11–17)

The great God Almighty is the God of history. And what will He do now?

See, I am doing a new thing!

Now it springs up; do you not
   perceive it?
I am making a way in the desert
   and streams in the wasteland.
The wild animals honor me,
   the jackals and the owls,
because I provide water in the desert
   and streams in the wasteland,
to give drink to my people, my chosen.
   (43:19–20)

I believe that God has some chosen ones, and that God wants to bring drink to His chosen ones. To bring this to our church, we need to do a few things. One is to repudiate unbelief. The average evangelical church lies under a shadow of quiet doubting. The doubt is not the unbelief that argues against Scripture, but worse than that. It is chronic unbelief that does not know what faith means.

There is a difference between the unbeliever who does not believe the Bible, boldly says so and argues against it and the so-called Christian who simply lies in a state of coma and cannot rise and believe. It is like the difference between a man who has had an accident or becomes suddenly ill and the chronic invalid who never knows what it is to be quite well, but who is not quite dead. The invalid can always muster a smile and does have a heartbeat, but the person is not normal. He does have a temperature and respiration, but he is not normal. The person is not alive, but, thank God, he is not dead, either.

The person who hits the abutment of the road doing 60 miles per hour is still warm although dead. Drag such a person out and he or she is still warm—but dead. Death happened suddenly and dramatically. Likewise, something dramatic and terrible has happened to the person who says, "I don't believe your Bible. It's a saga of old notions. It's filled with stories of adultery and murder and assassination. I don't believe your Bible." He or she has hit something hard and has been injured.

A state of chronic unbelief

But the churches lie around in a state of chronic unbelief. They do not expect God to do anything, and naturally He does not. On occasion one will be added to the church by mulling and wooing and needling and pawing over the person until we get him or her in. But the lift, freedom, brightness and joy of the true Christian who believes God is missing from us.

The voice of unbelief comes out of the psychology of nonexpectation. This is our trouble these days: the psychology of nonexpectation. So we sit down to have a board meeting. What are we going to do to stir ourselves up? Who can we get? Where will we look? We forget that all the time Jehovah is present. "I am *Jehovah-shammah*; I am in the midst of you. Why don't you talk to me?" No, we don't ask Him.

"I am your banner of victory." But we say, "I just wonder how much it will cost?" How much does a revival cost? Absolutely nothing and absolutely everything—that is how much it will cost. It will cost not one dime, and it will cost everything we have. You cannot import it by flying someone in from New Zealand. How many of these blessed preachers have come in from Ireland and England? They did some big things over there, we heard, so we flew them in and they never got anywhere. I never saw anything result from trying to import God. He does not fly over in a jet. He says, "I am Jehovah; I am with you. I am where you are; I am here now. Call on me."

"But you do not call on me," He says next. "Yet you have not called upon me, O Jacob, you have not wearied yourselves for me, O Israel" (Isaiah 43:22). In other words, we are bored with God Almighty. We chuckle at Pogo and laugh at Dear Abby, but we are bored with God. "You are weary of me; you are bored with me." I do not hesitate to say that much of what is going on in the name of Christianity today is simply boredom.

God says, "Why don't you call on me? I am here, and I am ready to help you. I will do these things for you." The voice of unbelief says, "Things will be as they are. There is no use." But the voice of Jehovah says, "I will do a new thing. I will make a way in the wilderness. I will make rivers in the desert."

Unbelief is entirely logical and true to nature. People of faith, however, have a logic that is higher than natural logic, a logic that cannot be seen by unbelievers. But unbelief is entirely logical. The sun rises, and the sun also sets. It rains and it snows. Seasons follow each other. The ducks fly to the north and then to the south. Babies are born and old men die. Things go on as they go on. "As it was in the beginning, is now and ever shall be"—that is the only hymn we know. Things will be as they have been, we sing in unbelief.

"Behold, I will"

But the voice of Jehovah says, "Behold, I will." When you introduce God, a new thing happens. "I will make a way in the wilderness." Who ever heard of it? "I will make rivers in the desert." Who ever heard of it? Unbelief is logical and true to nature because nature is fixed in a regular routine. You may expect nature to continue to go right on in that routine. However, another factor is now introduced. God introduces the supernatural, and He says, "I am who I am and I will." God wills to do a new thing.

We keep going the way of nature in the fixed routine. You cannot expect anybody to do anything about it. But I hear another voice saying, "I am who I am." Since I have been a Christian,

I have lived for that voice. I have lived to hear God say, "I am who I am. You can't, but I can. You aren't, but I am. You are not able, but I am able. You have no wisdom, but I am Jehovah and I have the wisdom."

We approach Him through Jesus Christ His Son. Never forget that all the power of this great Jehovah with His awful and awesome glorious names is channeled through the person of His Son, Jesus Christ, to His people. Jesus dug a channel, so to speak, through to the mighty ocean that is Jehovah so all the sweet waters, the healing waters, the soul-quenching waters that are God can flow down to the Lord's people if they would only believe.

God does not say that this is new to Him. Nothing is new to God; it is just new to us. When God says to us, "I will do a new thing," what is it? Is God going to create something brand new as though He were creating a galaxy out of nothing? No, He is going to repeat for a new generation what He did for an old generation. He says, "I will do it for you. Why do you worry? I will do it for you. I am God. I am Jehovah. I am your righteousness. I am your provider. I am your healer. I am your banner of victory. I am your shepherd. I am your peace. I am your everything."

If God is all this to us, then there is no reason why anybody should be downhearted in this hour. If God could make a world out of nothing, why can't He make anything He wants now for His people? God invites us to see Him work.

God will do it in such a way that nobody gets the glory but Himself. God is going to get the glory, and He is not going to share it with anybody. "I am Jehovah, and my glory I will not share with another." God wants to do things in a way that nobody can say somebody else did it. God is doing it because He wants the glory and must have the glory because of who He is. He says, "I will make." We need a God who can make things; we need a God who can create, and He invites us to watch Him create.

Don't allow past to paralyze you

Do not let any of the things of the world or past mistakes paralyze your hearts. I believe there are Christians who have allowed some of their past mistakes to paralyze them. You were so bright and cheerful in your spiritual life once, and then you made some tragic mistake or had something happen to you. You got out of it somehow, and prayed and wept your way out of it. But it did something to you, and now you cannot lick it. Past wrongs that have been done to you, past failures, times you thought you were going to win and did not, or present sins or discouragement—these things are not mental at all. They are deeper than that; they are subconscious, and they prevent us from believing.

I most urgently exhort you, and I trust God Almighty to deliver you; to sponge that out of your spirit; to sponge that out of your heart so you are not hindered by unbelief. The simple people of the world can believe God in a way that we who are more sophisticated have a hard time doing. That is why God has to begin with the simple people. Jesus could not get the Pharisees to follow Him, but He did get some fishermen and some simple people. He got one tax collector, but He did not get very many great people. God comes to simple people.

If we could shake off our sophistication, our pseudo learning and the cheap crust of unbelief that is over us, we could hear Him say, "I am that I am, and I am with you. I am on your side. My Son died for you, and hell cannot take you out of my hands. You are made for my glory. I formed you for myself to praise me. If you will only believe, I will give you waters in the wilderness and rivers in the desert. I will give drink to my people, my chosen. I will do these things for you."

An element of the supernatural enters here. Nature says it cannot be, and nature is right. But God steps in and says, "I am who I am, and it can be." And God is right. I cannot win against my enemies, but God says, "I will be an enemy to your enemies and an adversary to your adversaries."

If we will unite our hearts and intentions and dare to believe it, we will see God begin to move in great strength and in great power. We will see coming down from heaven that which we so desperately struggled to bring in from the outside. We will see the great God do it and then it will not be said, "This man did it," or "That woman did it." But we can all say together, " Not by might nor by power, but by my Spirit,' says the LORD Almighty" (Zechariah 4:6b).

The Great Test:
Modifying the Truth

There is a great decision that every denomination has to make sometime in the development of its history. Every church also has to make it either at its beginning or a little later—usually a little later. Eventually every board is faced with the decision and has to keep making it, not by one great decision made once for all, but by a series of little decisions adding up to one great big one. Every pastor has to face it and keep renewing his decision on his knees before God. Finally, every church member, every evangelist, every Christian has to make this decision. It is a matter of judgment upon that denomination, that church, that board, that pastor, that leader and upon their descendants and spiritual children.

The question is this: Shall we modify the truth in doctrine or practice to gain more adherents? Or shall we preserve the truth in doctrine and practice and take the consequences? If the decision is that we modify the truth and practice of the church, then we are responsible for the consequences, whatever they may be. God already knows what the consequences are, and history has shown what they are. But if we choose to preserve the truth, then God accepts the responsibility.

Business people have to make that choice in business. Everyone has to make it at income tax time. Students have to make it in school. We have to make it everywhere in our lives as we touch society. Shall we preserve the truth and the practice of the truth, or shall we alter it just comfortably in order to be more popular, gain more adherents and get along easier in the world?

Actually such a question should never need to be asked. It is like asking, "Should a man be faithful to his wife?" There is only one answer to that question. When we ask, "Shall we preserve the truth and practice of the church, or shall we modify it for immediate and visible results?" we ought to have only one answer. It is not a debatable question, and yet it is one that has to be constantly debated in the secret prayer chamber. It is constantly debated when conferences meet, when boards meet and when a pastor must make a decision.

A commitment to preserving the truth and practice of the church is what separates me from a great many people who are perhaps far greater than I am in ability. This is my conviction, long held and deeply confirmed by a

knowledge of the fact that modern gospel churches, almost without exception, have decided
to modify the truth and practice a little in order
to have more adherents and get along better.
When we make a decision to modify the truth,
we bring the consequences of that choice upon
ourselves. What have the consequences been?

One has been an absence of a spirit of worship in the church. Many people do not even
know what is meant by a spirit of worship.
That is tragic. I wish God would either change
things a little or give me a sight of His glory
among His people. I admit that sometimes I
feel like the man of God who said,

> Oh, that I had the wings of a dove!
> I would fly away and be at rest—
> I would flee far away
> and stay in the desert. (Psalm 55:6–7)

Many of the Lord's people do not know what
you mean when you mention a spirit of worship in the church. They are poor victims of
boards, churches, denominations and pastors
who have made the noble decision to modify
the truth and practice a little. But God
responded, "If you do, I will withdraw from
you the spirit of worship. I will remove your
candlestick."

Absence of spiritual desire

A second consequence is the absence of

spiritual desire. How many people do you know who are all burnt up with spiritual desire and longing after God? How many have tears of eagerness in their eyes when you talk to them? How many say, "Oh, that I might know God better!" Our fathers had spiritual desire, and they spent days with God.

Another result is coldness of heart, which is similar to an absence of spiritual desire. Once you have been baptized with the fire of inward longing, you will never be satisfied with coldness of heart.

G. Campbell Morgan, the great English preacher, went to Wales to see the Welsh revival and then came back to Westminster Chapel. What he saw in Wales so moved the great expositor that he got up and roundly lectured his audience. In effect he said, "You are a cold bunch. You don't even sing warmly; you don't even sing right." Morgan had heard the Welsh sing—they sang the Psalms and nothing else. A man would get up to preach, and in the audience somebody would raise a psalm and off the whole congregation would go, singing a psalm. The preacher would have to sit down in confusion. God had never told him to preach anyhow, and he knew it. Then two or three people would get down on their knees and get converted—no altar calls; they just got converted where they were. The fire of God would fall upon them everywhere.

One man got up and said, "I have a sermon

tonight that consists of three Cs," and he listed his three points each beginning with the letter C. Before he was halfway through the first C, the Holy Spirit fell on the audience. Somebody with a high voice raised a psalm, and they sang him down. He sat down with the other two Cs unmolested. Those people had warmth of heart. But we do not have it because we have made the ignoble decision that we would rather compromise a little bit on truth and practice.

Lack of spirit of prayer

A fourth consequence is the lack of the spirit of prayer. No child is born until there is labor. When Evan Roberts, whom God used to start the great Welsh revival, was in a prayer meeting somebody said to him, "Evan, never miss a prayer meeting, because the one you miss may be the one when the Holy Spirit falls." So Evan never missed a prayer meeting. One night when he was on his knees the Holy Spirit fell upon him, and he began to pray, "Oh God, bend me, bend me, bend me." Another man was praying, and Evan did not want to break in. Roberts described the experience, "I waited for the other man to get through, but it seemed he would never get through; he prayed on and on. Finally, he tapered off and petered out and said, 'Amen.'" Evan began to pray, and the place was shaken with his prayer. From there on the revival in Wales was under way.

Now that is the spirit of prayer. When the spirit of prayer falls on people, God answers their prayer and things are done. When a spirit of prayer is not on us, we just mumble on endlessly. But when the spirit of prayer is on us, the Spirit praying in us to the God above us will get things done around us.

No sense of God's presence

A fifth consequence of modifying the truth is that there is no sense of God's presence in the average church. I get around quite a bit, but I do not go into many places where I find the sense of God's presence. There are almost no answers to prayer and almost no divine manifestations. This leads to the deadliest consequence of all: the absence of saintliness.

There are a few saints around who are so sold out to God that you could not keep them still. They are always coming up with something, and you know that they have been in the presence of the Lord. They live their faith regularly and consistently. Everything they do is congruous with everything they testify to.

The spirit of worship should be on us until tears are as common as the snow over Toronto. It is the will of God that we should be burnt with spiritual desire. We should be singing, "Oh Jesus, Jesus, dearest Lord, forgive me if I say, for very love Thy precious name a thousand times a day." We would not be singing hypocritically—we would mean it.

It is God's will that we should have no coldness of heart. The difference between coldness of heart and warmth of heart is the difference between being in love and not being in love. When a person loves deeply, whether someone of the opposite sex or a baby or a child, it warms the affections. Sometimes our telephone rings at night, and the operator at the other end of the line says, "Would you receive this phone call, please, collect from somebody named Becky?" As soon as that call comes from my daughter I feel something warm inside. I get calls from people for whom I do not feel anything warm. Somebody usually wants me to do something. I like those people, but I am not particularly warm. That is the difference between coldness and warmth of heart.

God wants us to have warm hearts, and He wants us to have a spirit of prayer so prayer is effective. Most prayer is like forever turning a key on a dead battery, and the starter does not even whine. Turn the key for 20 minutes saying, "Our Lord and our Father . . . " 29 times, and there is still not a buzz. God does not want us to pray like that. He wants a spirit of prayer to be on the people. You can have that spirit of prayer. He wants to answer your prayer, and He wants the sense of His presence to be upon you. Always remember one thing: When the Spirit of the Lord comes, that is the presence, and you have that presence. God does want to manifest Himself.

Our eagerness to be proper, never get out of order and never have anything fanatical happen continues until nothing happens at all. There is no divine manifestation, and there is an absence of saintliness. Yet God wants us to know His presence and exhibit saintliness.

Usually follow a trend

How did we get into this fix that we are in? Well, evangelicals usually follow a trend. It is dangerous to follow a trend unless your eyes are open and you know where the trend is going. This trend began in the last decades of the last century and carried on with some big names promoting it. In their zeal to make converts and adherents, they oversimplified the Christian faith. That is our difficulty today. We oversimplify it, and yet we never get simple. Isn't that odd? We oversimplify the truth, and yet we have the most complex, mixed up beliefs.

The average Christian is like a kitten that has found a ball of yarn and has played with the yarn and romped until it is wrapped in a cocoon. The kitten cannot get itself out. It just lies there and whimpers. Somebody has to come unwind it. We have tried to be simple, but instead of being simple we have simplified—we have not become simple. We are sophisticated and overly complex.

We have simplified so Christianity amounts to this: God is love; Jesus died for you; believe, accept, be jolly, have fun and tell others. And away we go—that is the Christianity of our day. I would not give a plug nickel for the whole business of it. Once in a while God has a poor bleeding sheep that manages to live on that kind of thing and we wonder how.

I have traveled through the American Southwest, and I have seen swaybacked cattle. You could count every rib if the train was not going too fast. They stand out there between stalks of long grass, brown and dry and hard. As we sailed by on a fast, streamlined train, I wondered how the poor things ever live. Somehow or other they manage to do it.

You will find a few of God's people here and there even in that kind of atmosphere. Whole generations of Christians have grown up believing that this is the faith of our fathers living still, in spite of dungeons, fire and sword. The devil would not be caught dead trying to kill anybody for acting like that. It does not bother him—the only thing the devil hates is somebody who is after him.

When my friend Alan Redpath shakes your hand to say goodbye, he smiles and says, "Well, K.O.K.T.D." That stands for "keep on kicking the devil." The devil does not mind if you are not a bother to him, and most of us are not. The devil looks at us, smiles and says, "That poor little emaciated weakling can't do my kingdom any harm." A whole generation has thought this to be Christianity. That is the faith of our fathers, living still, in spite of dungeon fire and sword. Nobody ever put people like that in a dungeon—they are already there. They were born into it. Nobody ever threw them to the flames, because they are harmless.

There must come a reformation, a revival that will result in a fresh emphasis on neglected truth. I do not preach any new truth. I do not have a new doctrine, and if anybody would come here preaching a new doctrine, I would say, "I'm sorry, but we already have our doctrine." I would not allow that preacher in the pulpit. We do not want new doctrine—we want fresh emphasis on doctrine already well known by all of us.

Revival that will mean purity of heart

We must have a revival that will mean purity of heart as a normal standard for everybody. We must be clean people, and not only clean outside. Average evangelicals do not smoke, and because they do not, they feel they are doing God's service. Thank God they do not smoke—that is a start toward clean living. But purity of heart goes deeper.

Purity of heart is taken for granted, yet we must have it to be clean people. Even in my lifetime—and I have not lived 500 years yet—I can well remember that when people lost their tempers they had to go to an altar and get cleansed. People knew they were out of victory and were not right with God. People were supposed to have a pure heart. We need and must have a revival that will mean divine energy to give our Christian witness power.

"You will receive power when the Holy Spirit comes on you; and you will be my witnesses" (Acts 1:8a). It is frustrating to talk to people about the Lord and not get anywhere at all, to not have any power at all.

In addition to becoming people with clean hearts, we must become a fellowship where there are frequent answers to prayer and the calling out of Christian missionaries and preachers. I would like to see our young people feel the call of God on them until they have to leave us and begin preaching. I would like to see the Spirit of God move upon us until our young people cannot afford to sit and figure out who they are going to marry and when. That will come in its time, but they will be thinking, *Where can I serve God?* Then one day, suddenly, the hand of God will be laid on their shoulders and off they will go. How many young people like that have I seen? Many young people do come to me and say, "I feel that God has His hand on me."

A man I knew during World War II was something of an oddball in temperament. I never thought he would amount to very much. He went off to the war, was wounded and was tumbling over a cliff. He would have fallen to his death below. Before he went over he said, "I am called to Ethiopia." As he was tumbling and sliding slowly toward certain death, he knew he was called to Ethiopia. A great big old tough sergeant saw him, grabbed him as he was going over and hauled him back, and he recovered. He came back after the war but nobody wanted him; he did not have the proper schooling. Finally, a well-known missionary society sent him to Ethiopia. He went over there and has been preaching there ever since.

We need revival and reformation

I believe we desperately need revival and reformation to come. In Exodus they came to the end of 400 years of Israel's defeat. I read of Hezekiah, the son of an evil father, Ahaz, who had brought Israel to the lowest moral condition that it had been in for a long time. Ahaz died and his son Hezekiah reigned in his stead. Hezekiah was a holy man and sought God immediately. He threw the dirt out of the temple and sent word throughout all Israel and said, "Come to the meeting." Israel began to be blessed. They cleansed the temple and started the fires again. The first thing they knew they had a revival on their hands. It was also Hezekiah who prayed when Sennacherib came down like a wolf on a foal with his cohorts all gleaming in purple and gold. It was under Hezekiah that the breath of the Lord smote those thousands and delivered Jerusalem.

When the Israelites returned from Babylon

God spoke to a man who cared, a man with a concern, who was cupbearer to the king. The king said, "What's the matter with you? You haven't been gloomy like this before." Nehemiah responded, "Your majesty, pardon me please, but I can't help it. My heart is broken. My father's city is in rubble and the foxes run over the walls. The glorious temple where we used to worship Jehovah has been razed to the ground and the religion of Israel is gone into decay." King Artaxerxes, not knowing that God was working in his life, said, "You go back to rebuild Jerusalem." That was the beginning of the return from Babylon.

Since Bible times we have had these periods of refreshing from the presence of the Lord. I just happened to notice a comment in a book I was reading today on this subject. The writer said, "God added a postscript to that." Here it is: "He who has an ear, let him hear what the Spirit says to the churches. To him who overcomes, I will give the right to eat from the tree of life, which is in the paradise of God" (Revelation 2:7).

Everyone has a private battle going on, a private fight. You are in the midst of a wicked and adulterous generation, but you have got to overcome. He who overcame indicates that you also can overcome, but He indicates that not all do. You can overcome your own flesh, which will be the hardest. You can overcome tradition and custom, which will be the second hardest.

You can overcome all things. "To him who overcomes, I will give the right to eat from the tree of life, which is in the paradise of God" (2:7b).

The world is waiting to hear an authentic voice, a voice from God—not an echo of what others are doing and saying, but an authentic voice.

HODDER CHRISTIAN ESSENTIALS

- **Esteemed Authors**
- **Essential Subjects**
- **Excellent Value**

Beyond Ourselves by Catherine Marshall
Our relationship with God

The Empty Cross of Jesus by Michael Green
The crucifixion and resurrection

Fear No Evil by David Watson
Faith in the face of death

The Gift of Giving by R T Kendall
What it means to tithe

God has Spoken by J I Packer
Reading God's word

The Gravedigger Files by Os Guinness
The threats facing the Church

The Hard Sayings of Jesus by F F Bruce
Explaining the most difficult gospel sayings

The Helper by Catherine Marshall
The work of the Holy Spirit

I Am Not Ashamed by Martin Lloyd-Jones
Rejoicing in the good news of the gospel

Loving God by Charles Colson
Obeying the first commandment

One in the Spirit by David Watson
The work of the Holy Spirit

Out of the Rut, Into Revival by A W Tozer
The need for renewal, and how to find it

Prayers and Promises for Every Day by Corrie ten Boom
The fulfilment of God's promises in our lives

This Day is the Lord's by Corrie ten Boom
Daily meditations to renew our faith

SOME BESTSELLERS FROM
HODDER CHRISTIAN BOOKS

THE HIDING PLACE by Corrie ten Boom

The triumphant story of Corrie ten Boom, heroine of the anti-Nazi underground.

"A brave and heartening story."

Baptist Times

GOD'S SMUGGLER by Brother Andrew

An international bestseller. God's Smuggler carries contraband Bibles past armed border guards to bring the love of Christ to the people behind the Iron Curtain.

"A book you will not want to miss."

Catherine Marshall

DISCIPLESHIP by David Watson

". . . breath-taking, block-busting, Bible-based simplicity on every page."

Jim Packer

LISTENING TO GOD by Joyce Huggett

A profound spiritual testimony, and practical help for discovering a new dimension of prayer.

"This is counselling at its best."

Leadership Today

CELEBRATION OF DISCIPLINE by Richard Foster

A classic on the Spiritual Disciplines.

"For any Christian hungry for teaching, I would recommend this as being one of the most challenging books to have been published."

Delia Smith

RUN BABY RUN by Nicky Cruz with Jamie Buckingham

A tough New York gang leader discovers Christ.

"It is a thrilling story. My hope is that it shall have a wide reading."

Billy Graham

CHASING THE DRAGON by Jackie Pullinger with Andrew Quicke

Life-changing miracles in Hong Kong's Walled City.

"A book to stop you in your tracks."

Liverpool Daily Post

BORN AGAIN by Charles Colson

Disgraced by Watergate, Charles Colson finds a new life.

"An action packed story of real life drama and a revelation of modern history as well as a moving personal account."

Elim Evangel

KNOWING GOD by J I Packer

The biblical portrait that has become a classic.

"(The author) illumines every doctrine he touches and commends it with courage, logic, lucidity and warmth . . . the truth he handles fires the heart. At least it fired mine, and compelled me to turn aside to worship and pray."

John Stott

THE HAPPIEST PEOPLE ON EARTH by
Demos Shakarian with John and Elizabeth Sherrill

The extraordinary beginnings of the Full Gospel Business Men's Fellowship.